Contents

"The universe is full of magical things, patiently waiting for our wits to grow sharper."

— Eden Phillpotts

1. Unveiling the Mystic Leaves: An Introduction to Emacs Fortune Telling

In the world of ancient divination and modern technology, there exists a unique fusion that combines the enigmatic art of tea leaf reading with the cerebral power of Emacs—a versatile, code-editing software beloved by programmers. "The Tea Leaf Guide: Emacs Fortune Telling" invites you on an intriguing journey where mysticism meets elegance through the medium of technology and tradition. Whether you're a seasoned coder curious about the mystical worlds or a fortune enthusiast ready to explore digital realms, this book offers a comprehensive guide that demystifies the art of tasseography using the powerful tool that is Emacs. As you turn these pages, prepare to blend the serenity of a tea ritual with the analytical prowess of Emacs to unravel insights about past, present, and future aspirations. Let's delve into this captivating synthesis of old and new, inspiring creativity along the way.

2. History of Tea Leaf Reading and Its Cultural Roots

2.1. The Origins of Tasseography

The origins of tasseography, or tea leaf reading, can be traced back to various ancient practices and beliefs surrounding the consumption of tea, with deep roots that intertwine with cultural rituals and spiritual interpretations. The art of interpreting symbols formed by tea leaves left in a cup emerged as an intuitive practice, growing from the simple act of drinking tea into a complex divination method.

Historical records indicate that tea itself was first cultivated in China, with artifacts suggesting consumption of tea dating back to as early as 2737 BCE. The Chinese revered tea not merely as a beverage but as a conduit of health, wellness, and philosophical pursuits. As the tea culture expanded, it found its way into various other cultures, bringing with it diverse interpretations and rituals tied to fortune telling.

In its early stages, the practice of tasseography was closely linked to the concept of synchronicity — the belief that events occurring in the natural world resonate with the internal states of individuals. Therefore, the patterns formed by tea leaves were believed to symbolize not only the drinker's current state of being but also hints of what the future might hold. Various interpretations emerged, and readers began to develop a lexicon of shapes and symbols derived from common motifs found in the residual leaves.

Tracking the cultural influences on tasseography, the Greeks contributed to the evolution of divinatory practices, merging Hellenistic methods with those acquired from Eastern practices. Notably, they employed various forms of mediumistic readings, often utilizing symbolic translations that resonated with tea leaves' disjointed shapes. Revering the mysterious nature of fate and the individual's ability to gain insights from tea leaves, they encouraged the method's establishment.

In the medieval era, the practice began to migrate westward, reaching Europe during the 17th century with the increasing popularity of tea among European elites. The aristocracy embraced tea drinking as a fashionable pastime, leading to a blend of sociable gatherings and mystical practices. During this time, a fascination with the occult flourished, and tasseography made its way into social parlors, becoming a common entertainment at gatherings. It was not merely an attempt to foresee the future but also a social ritual that encouraged connections between people through shared experiences of divination.

Various cultural adaptations emerged from this integration into European society. In France, specially designed cups for tea reading gained popularity; these cups often featured demarcated symbols and images that were thought to enhance interpretations. Similarly, in the United Kingdom, tea leaf readings gained a firm footing in the Victorian belief system that emphasized intuition and personal insight.

The 19th century marked a significant rise in published literature dedicated to tasseography. Authors began compiling guides and manuals that mapped out symbols and their meanings, effectively codifying the practice. The art of tea leaf reading thus transformed into a method that combined both intuitive reading and structured interpretation, allowing novice readers to engage with the practice more effectively.

As the modern era dawned, regardless of cultural background, the symbols interpreted from tea leaves took on subjective meanings related to personal experiences and societal influences. Within this context, tea leaf reading transcended mere divination; it became a means for individuals to connect to their collective history, shaping identities through interpretation. The narratives crafted from these symbols offered reflectiveness not just about personal lives, but broader societal dynamics adopted across various communities.

In contemporary settings, the advent of technology has injected new life into the ancient practice of tasseography, prompting discussions about how traditional methods can coexist with modern technologies. This juxtaposition raises questions about the essence of divination: is it the medium that matters, or the act of interpretation itself? The fusion of tea leaf reading and technology, particularly through platforms like Emacs, ushers in a new chapter in the history of tasseography.

Today, the practice of tea leaf reading is experiencing a revival compounded by the rise of mindfulness and holistic wellness movements. People are increasingly seeking out practices that honor both their heritage and aspirations for self-discovery. The blend of ancient traditions with innovative platforms signals an exciting evolution, one that fosters creativity, community, and self-reflection.

Through this exploration of its origins, it becomes clear that tassaography is more than a divinatory practice—it embodies a rich tapestry of history, culture, and personal connection. As we dive deeper into the nuances of tea leaf reading, we find ourselves not just engaged in a ritualistic practice, but also participating in an ongoing conversation that bridges the past, connects with the present, and opens pathways to the future. The leaves may tell the story, but it is the reader's interpretation that brings those stories to life, framing them in the context of both the individual and the collective experience.

2.2. Cultural Significance Across the Globe

Tea leaf reading, or tasseography, transcends mere entertainment; it embodies a rich tradition woven into the cultural fabric of societies across the globe. Each culture has embraced and adapted this ancient art, infusing it with local flavors, beliefs, and practices that reflect their unique worldviews.

In Asia, where the practice originated, tea holds a significant cultural and spiritual role. In China, tasseography is not simply a method of divination; it intertwines with philosophies like Daoism and Buddhism, embracing concepts of fate and the interconnectedness of life. Traditionally, after enjoying a pot of tea, one would leave a small amount in their cup and turn it upside down. The patterns formed by the remaining leaves would then provide insights into one's future, aligning with the Daoist belief in the flow of fate. In some regions, experienced tea readers could discern the weather and other natural phenomena through the shapes of leaves—a testament to the profound connection between humans and their environment.

Traveling to Japan, we find another cultural variant. The Japanese practice of tea ceremony, or Chanoyu, emphasizes mindfulness and harmony. While traditional readings aren't as commonplace, the ceremonial aspects of tea align perfectly with the meditative qualities of tea leaf reading. In this context, it's less about predicting the future and more about engaging with the present, cultivating awareness, and exploring the symbolic language of nature. The shapes in the cup can be seen as reflections of one's current emotional state rather than fixed outcomes, suggesting that tea reading in Japan serves as a tool for introspective practice.

As we move to the Middle East, specifically Iran, tea drinking is a foundational aspect of hospitality and social connection. While not widely known for tasseography, the act of pouring tea in specific ways to reveal the subtle flavors parallels the philosophy behind reading tea leaves. Community gatherings often involve shared cups, where personal and shared stories emerge—much like readings where insights foster connections among participants. The social dynamics inherent in tea sharing in this region enhance the interpretative opportunity, embodying a collective approach to divination.

In Western cultures, especially during the 18th and 19th centuries, tea leaf reading became a popular societal pastime amongst the gentry. It was embraced not only as a divinatory practice but as a means of social engagement. Tea parties provided a cozy backdrop for gathering friends, where fortunes were told amidst laughter and conversation. The symbols interpreted during these readings often reflected contemporary aspirations and anxieties, speaking to the time's collective psyche. For example, in Victorian England, the emphasis on social propriety was echoed in readings that focused on themes of love, marriage, and status.

In contemporary Native American traditions, some tribes have explored fortune-telling practices that resonate with the essence of tasseography. While traditional methods may vary, the integrity of the earth, nature, and spirituality underpin these adaptations. Engaging with tea leaves can serve as an avenue for connecting with ancestral wisdom, allowing practitioners to interpret patterns steeped in cultural significance that resonate with their life experiences and history.

Likewise, in Africa, traditional divination practices such as Ifá and others take precedence, where materials reveal insights through deeply embedded symbolic meanings. The global tea culture, however, has created a pathway for innovating reading styles that marry local indigenous methods with the artistry of tasseography. The emergence of blended ceremonies invites diverse cultural interpretations, fostering a rich dialogue that enhances the traditional understanding of both tea and divinatory practices.

In recent years, the digital age has profoundly shifted how traditions like tasseography are experienced and shared. Social media platforms have allowed for a cross-cultural convergence, where practitioners from various backgrounds share techniques, interpretations, and personal stories related to tea leaf readings. This digital sharing cultivates a vibrant, dynamic community of enthusiasts who appreciate the historical contexts of their practices while contributing their unique cultural narratives. This global fusion not only keeps ancient traditions alive but enriches them through the interplay of modern perspectives.

As we continue to witness the integration of technology and ancient practices, it is essential to recognize the dialogues occurring in contemporary settings. Embracing new techniques while respecting traditional methods allows for a broader understanding of tea leaf reading's cultural significance. The diverse interpretations stemming from various backgrounds remind us that while the leaves create shapes, it is the unique lens of each culture that breathes life into their meanings.

Acknowledge the rich tapestry woven through the ages by tea leaf reading, and embrace the understanding that it is as much about personal identity and cultural heritage as it is about divination itself. By exploring these cultural intersections, we not only honor the past but also invite new generations to partake in this mystical art, ensuring its continued relevance and appreciation across borders and boundaries. Each cup of tea presents an opportunity—an invitation to engage with history, culture, and personal insight, all entwined in the simple yet profound act of reading the leaves.

2.3. Myths and Legends Surrounding Tea Leaves

Throughout history, tea leaves have been enveloped in an alluring aura of mystique, giving rise to a multitude of myths and legends that enrich the practice of tasseography. These narratives, often steeped in cultural significance, have helped shape individual interpretations and experiences surrounding tea leaf reading, lending a sense of depth to the seemingly simple act of enjoying a cup of tea. Exploring these tales allows us to understand not only the enduring appeal of tea leaves as tools for divination but also the deeper human desires for connection, understanding, and insight into the unknown.

One of the most enduring myths surrounding tea leaves is that they possess a supernatural ability to reveal the secrets of the universe. This belief can be traced back to ancient civilizations where tea was regarded not just as a beverage, but as a divine elixir conferred with mystical properties. Legends abound of wise sages who could gaze into the swirling depths of their cups and divine the fates of those around them. These storytellers held sacred responsibilities, entrusted with guiding communities through the tumultuous waters of life by revealing knowledge said to be granted by higher powers. Stories of these sages became so woven into cultural landscapes that the act of tea leaf reading evolved into a spiritual rite, believed to bridge the gap between the material and the divine.

In various cultures, the themes surrounding tea leaves often encompass the four elements: earth, water, fire, and air. Mythology asserts that when tea leaves settle in a cup, they mirror cosmic forces in motion. For instance, water symbolizes feelings and intuition, while earth represents stability and growth. Fire signifies transformation and passion, and air embodies intellect and communication. The shapes formed by the leaves in the cup are said to capture a snapshot of the drinker's life at that very moment, serving as a reflection of their inner world harmonized with the forces of the universe. This interplay between the elements allows readers to decipher guidance that is both personal and universal.

In numerous folk tales, tea leaves are also described as messengers from the spirits of loved ones or ancestors. Practitioners often speak of receiving clear images or familiar symbols that invoke memories of those who have passed. These encounters are seen as a testament to the belief that even in death, our loved ones remain close, offering counsel and love through the medium of tea leaves. It is a poignant reminder that tea leaf reading can serve as a link between generations, providing solace and comfort while celebrating the legacy of those who came before.

Another powerful legend resides in the belief of transformation and renewal tied to the experience of drinking tea. Tales abound of individuals who, after participating in a tea leaf reading, undergo significant life changes sparked by the insights gained during the ritual. Stories recount how interpretations leading to self-discovery have empowered people to change careers, launch creative endeavors, or initiate relationships. The act of reading tea leaves becomes a metaphorical initiation, a rite of passage that encourages individuals to embark on new journeys and redefine their lives. This transformative narrative closely mirrors human experiences, suggesting that the potential for change is intrinsic to the act of divination.

In modern interpretations, the myths surrounding tea leaves have adapted to accommodate contemporary society's values and ideals. The reception of exorbitantly intricate tea leaf symbols in pop culture emphasizes not only entertainment but also personal empowerment. Social media platforms have galvanized communities to share their mystical tea experiences, transcending traditional beliefs and intertwining them with modern aspirations for self-improvement and self-discovery. The digital age has redefined tea leaf reading, allowing unique angles and approaches to emerge while retaining the ancient myths that underline its practice.

Additionally, the alignment with femininity is another recurring theme across myths associated with tea leaf reading. In many historical contexts, women have been the primary practitioners of this art, using it as a means of empowerment during periods when their voices were hushed. These tales echo through generations, celebrating the wisdom and strength of women who have relied on tea leaf reading as a tool for guidance and decision-making. From traditional tea circles to modern feminist interpretations, the act of reading tea leaves serves as an affirmation of feminine power and intuition.

As we consider these many myths and legends woven around tea leaves, we can appreciate how they enrich the practice of tasseography. These stories offer personal and collective meanings that resonate with readers across cultures and time. They remind us that tea is more than a beverage; it is a medium for connection, understanding, and exploration. Each reading invites us to tap into our intuition, reflect upon our experiences, and embrace the mysteries of existence intertwined with the narratives of humanity.

In conclusion, the myths and legends surrounding tea leaves are not merely tales of magic and prophecy; they mirror fundamental human experiences and aspirations. They encapsulate the longing for insight, the desire for connection, and the pursuit of transformation that embodies the journey of life. Supporting these myths are the vibrant cultures that have, for centuries, turned to tea leaves as guides, storytellers, and companions through the intricate tapestry of existence. By acknowledging these narratives, we cultivate a deeper connection to the practice of tea leaf reading, allowing the ancient art to thrive through new lenses of interpretation while honoring its storied past.

2.4. Symbolism in Historical Contexts

Throughout history, symbols have played a significant role in tea leaf reading, or tasseography, guiding the interpretation of the messages hidden within the swirling remnants of tea leaves. Understanding these symbols requires a keen awareness of the historical contexts in which they evolved, as meanings often vary widely across cultures and time periods. Each symbol is laden with cultural nuances, reflecting the beliefs, experiences, and aspirations of the people who interpreted them.

Ancient practices surrounding tea leaves were steeped in symbolism tied to natural elements, spiritual beliefs, and cultural traditions. In China, the cradle of tea culture, tea leaves symbolized much more than personal insight; they evoked connections to nature and the cosmos, a reflection of Daoist and Confucian philosophies. Shapes crafted by tea leaves were seen as ethereal messages from the universe, each curve and angle packed with potential meanings. For example, a leaf shaped like a mountain could symbolize stability and support, while a spiral might indicate a journey or transformation.

As tasseography traveled westward, particularly during the 17th and 18th centuries, its embrace shifted to accommodate various European traditions. The spiritual undertones from Asian practices began to blend with the social aspects of tea-drinking in the West. In Victorian England, for instance, tea leaf reading became a popular pastime among the upper classes, where it was not only a method of divination but also a means of fostering social connections. The symbols interpreted in these readings often reflected societal concerns, aspirations, and moral values of the era. A heart shape, for example, could indicate love or emotional connections, signaling the importance of marriage and romantic pursuits in Victorian society.

In this historical milieu, the significance of symbols expanded alongside cultural narratives. Different symbols emerged, driven by the common experiences and concerns of the time. The "cup overflowing" symbol, for instance, could indicate abundance or generosity, but during periods of economic uncertainty, it might also signify the querent's fears about resource management. Such readings framed individuals' personal stories within broader societal contexts, illuminating how collective experiences shape the interpretation of individual symbols.

Myths also colored the symbolism associated with tea leaves. Stories from various cultures describe tea leaves as celestial communicators or as carriers of ancestral wisdom. For instance, in some Native American traditions, divination practices emphasize the symbolism of nature and spirit guides, reflecting a profound respect for interpretive symbolism as a means of connecting past wisdom with present understanding. Such narratives reinforce the idea that symbols can carry messages across generations, holding layers of wisdom that contribute to the reader's personal journey and connections to their heritage.

In contemporary readings, the evolution of symbol interpretation continues to reflect modern anxieties and aspirations. While many traditional symbols remain intact, new interpretations have emerged to fit modern contexts. The advent of technology, for instance, has imbued certain shapes with new meanings, incorporating ideas from contemporary life. A laptop symbol appearing in the tea leaves might suggest guidance regarding digital communication or modern relationships, showcasing how the layering of symbols adapts to reflect current experiences.

Embracing symbols in their historical contexts allows practitioners to enrich their readings by understanding how the meanings have transformed and evolved. Historical contexts provide a deeper comprehension of the cultural significance behind each symbol, which fosters an enriching dialogue between the reader, their culture, and the personal contexts of their lives. When readers recognize that symbols resonate with both collective and individual histories, they deepen their connection to the practice as a tool for personal and community insight.

Furthermore, as individuals engage with technology in the modern age, the fusion of traditional symbols with digital platforms like Emacs opens new pathways for interpretation. Utilizing Emacs for organizing, documenting, and analyzing these symbols allows readers to blend ancient practices with contemporary methodologies, ensuring that interpretations remain relevant. By integrating historical understanding with modern techniques, practitioners can not only continue the legacy of tasseography but also adapt it to the evolving landscape of human experience.

Thus, the journey through the world of symbolic meanings in tasseography reflects a continuous dialogue across time, culture, and personal identity. Each reading becomes a tapestry woven from the threads of history and contemporary life, highlighting that the interpretations of symbols are not static. Instead, they exist within a dynamic continuum, encouraging readers to explore and discover new insights about themselves and the world around them. Ultimately, the symbols rendered by tea leaves invite curiosity, reflection, and a deeper appreciation for the intertwining of past and present within each reading experience.

2.5. The Evolution of Tasseography Practices

Tasseography, often described as the art of tea leaf reading, has a history marked by a remarkable evolution throughout the ages. Its journey from an ancient divinatory practice to a modern exploration of self-discovery and mindfulness reflects profound cultural shifts and interpretations fueled by societal changes and technological advancements. Chronicling this evolution reveals not only the dynamic nature of tea leaf reading but also the deeper human desire for connection, reflection, and understanding in an ever-changing world.

In its earliest manifestations, tasseography emerged deeply rooted in the traditions and spiritual beliefs of various cultures, particularly in Asia. For many, the ritual of tea drinking was not merely a source of nourishment but an act of communion with nature and the universe —a ceremonial observance deeply intertwined with philosophical ideals. Ancient Chinese practices emphasized the relationship between tea and the natural elements, where leaves left in the cup would form patterns that mirrored life's flow. This belief in synchronicity perpetuated the idea that the shapes left by tea leaves carried messages about one's destiny, aspirations, and emotional state.

As the art of tasseography spread to other cultures, its methods and interpretations began to diversify. Each culture adapted the practice, injecting local meanings and societal ideals that reflected their unique worldviews. In Europe, particularly during the 17th and 18th centuries, tea leaf reading became immensely popular among the upper classes. It evolved from an esoteric practice of divination into social entertainment, where individuals gathered to share readings, fostering communal bonds. This shift highlighted a significant transformation—the practice was no longer isolated to personal contemplation but became a shared experience that connected participants through storytelling and relational dynamics.

In the Victorian era, the fascination with tea leaf reading reached new heights, with an emphasis on structured interpretations and symbolic meanings that resonated with societal annotations on love, status, and personal fulfillment. Ladies and gentlemen of high society often engaged in this practice during tea parties, where interpretations mirrored concerns of the day. This era marked the solidification of baked-in symbolism—shapes such as hearts for love or keys for new opportunities became codified meanings that many readers adhered to, reflecting more than just personal insight but also societal consciousness influenced by class and gender.

The 19th century saw a proliferation of printed manuals dedicated to tasseography, solidifying these interpretations and providing guidelines for practitioners, which formalized the practice. This written aspect of gazing into tea leaves marked a significant transition, as it moved the art form from oral traditions into the realm of documentation and analysis, relics of a time when literacy and printed material became a gateway to knowledge for the masses. Consequently, this change brought both accessibility and limitations to the practice, as individuals began navigating readings more through structured systems rather than relying solely on intuition.

As societal paradigms shifted, particularly through the approaches carried by globalization and modernism in the 20th century, the interpretation of symbols grew more nuanced. The emergence of post-industrial spirituality emphasized self-discovery, where tea leaf reading transcended mere fortune-telling to become a tool for deeper introspection and mindfulness. Tasseography practitioners began to lean away from strict symbolic frameworks and instead prioritize the individual reader's personal connection with the shapes they interpreted, allowing space for subjective meanings derived from their own experiences and thoughts.

Simultaneously, the correlation between tea and mental wellness surged, prompting readers to embrace the therapeutic dimensions of tasseography. The act of drinking tea itself began to be acknowledged as a meditative process, where the interplay between the warmth of the beverage and the mindfulness of observing the residual leaves fostered a tranquil space for contemplation. This shift combined with growing societal interests in holistic well-being, spirituality, and personalized guidance reflected a responsiveness to the contemporary need for connection within a fast-paced modern backdrop.

In the present digital age, the integration of technology has been revolutionary for tasseography. With the advent of social media and online communities, tea leaf reading has experienced a resurgence, encouraging collaboration and collective exploration rarely seen before. Digital platforms allow practitioners to share their unique interpretations, techniques, and experiences, fostering a global dialogue that transcends geographical borders. As readers post photographs of their readings, detailed interpretations, and instructional content online, the art form not only flourishes through creative expression but also invites new interpretations that may blend traditional ideas with modern societal challenges.

Moreover, the intersection of technology extends into the use of software such as Emacs, which has fostered an innovative approach to managing and interpreting readings. The adaptation of coding skills to create personalized digital tools for documenting readings empowers practitioners to engage not just with the mystical side of tasseography but to intertwine it with analytical methodologies—a testament to merging creativity with structured thought. This duality within the contemporary practice enhances the way practitioners interact with symbols, explore messages, and self-reflect upon their journey.

Looking toward the future of tasseography, it is evident that the practice will continue to evolve, parallel to broader cultural themes and advancements. The democratization of information and experiences in our digital landscape allows for a continuous cross-pollination of ideas, shapes, and interpretations that can enrich the practice. New technologies may pave the way for innovative reading formats and community engagements, facilitating a fusion of ancient practices with modern sensibilities.

As we examine this journey from traditional sachet into both personal and communal pathways influenced by culture, societal norms, and technology, it becomes clear that the evolution of tasseography embodies the human capacity for connection, meaning-making, and self-discovery. Ultimately, whether through the richness of tea leaves or the precision of software, the spirit of tasseography endures—a reverent acknowledgment of the complex tapestry of life and the stories that unfold with each reading. In essence, the leaves may whisper their secret tales, yet it is the reader who breathes life into those stories, transforming the ancient craft into a vibrant conversation that bridges the mystical and the tangible.

3. Introduction to Emacs: A Programmer's Tool

3.1. What is Emacs?

Emacs is a highly customizable and extensible text editor that has garnered a loyal following among programmers and tech professionals. Known for its powerful capabilities, Emacs offers a seamless environment for editing code, writing documents, and even managing processes—all while boasting a robust set of features that can adapt to nearly any workflow.

At its core, Emacs is not just a simple text editor; it serves as a full integrated development environment (IDE) that supports multiple programming languages, syntax highlighting, and automated code folding. Emacs provides its users with a suite of powerful tools that extend beyond mere text manipulation to include version control systems, debugging tools, and project management functionalities. This versatility has made Emacs a favorite among those who seek a unified command center for their coding and writing tasks.

One of the defining characteristics of Emacs is its emphasis on customization. From the moment users launch the application, they encounter an environment that can be adapted to fit individual preferences. This customization can manifest in various ways— from changing color schemes and keybindings to integrating third-party libraries and tools. By utilizing Emacs' built-in configuration file, .emacs or init.el, users can script their own commands, create macros, and leverage various packages to enhance their experience. This reflects a fundamental philosophy of Emacs: anything can be adapted or created to meet personal needs.

In addition to its extensive customization options, Emacs boasts a wide range of extensions, or packages, available through repositories such as MELPA (Milkypostman's Emacs Lisp Package Archive). Whether one is looking for tools to optimize their workflow—like Org mode for organizing notes—or packages that provide enhanced programming experience—such as Magit for Git integration—there is a veritable treasure trove of resources available to enhance the Emacs experience. The community-driven development model encourages continuous innovation, which means users can expect regular updates and new features.

The interface of Emacs is unique and may initially seem daunting to new users. Instead of traditional, mouse-driven graphical interfaces, Emacs operates predominantly through keyboard shortcuts, making it particularly suited for users who prefer speed and efficiency in their workflows. This design choice can take some getting used to, but once users acclimatize, they often find that they can navigate and manipulate their environment with impressive speed and flexibility. Mastery of the keyboard commands can unlock a level of productivity that traditional GUI-based editors simply cannot match, and many users report that they become more proficient as they transition to this more keyboard-oriented approach.

Emacs also distinguishes itself through its cross-platform functionality. Being a software that runs on Windows, macOS, and Linux, it enables seamless transitions between different systems without requiring users to learn a plethora of different tools. This is especially appealing for those who frequently switch between machines or work in heterogeneous computing environments. The familiar interface and consistent behavior across platforms allow users to maintain continuity in their work, effortlessly picking up where they left off, regardless of the system they are using.

In addition to traditional coding tasks, Emacs has become a hub for non-programming activities, including writing documents, managing tasks, and even engaging in creative endeavors. Features like Org mode allow users to take notes, schedule tasks, and maintain to-do lists using a plaintext format that is supremely organized. The simplicity yet power of Emacs makes it an ideal choice for writers, researchers, and anyone needing to keep track of complex information.

Furthermore, Emacs has made significant strides towards integrating with modern technology. For instance, it can act as a client for email management, facilitate online collaborations, and integrate with popular cloud services. This flexibility allows Emacs to thrive in environments where flexibility and integration are key.

As we consider the intersection of Emacs and tasseography, it becomes apparent that the capabilities of Emacs can enhance the experience of tea leaf reading in profound ways. The ability to document and analyze readings, customize symbol libraries, and even connect to external resources presents an opportunity to blend the ancient art of divination with modern programming techniques and digital tools.

In conclusion, Emacs represents a unique platform that arises from the intersection of rich tradition and modern technological innovation. It serves as a versatile tool that accommodates both the analytical mind of the programmer and the creative spirit of the artist. Whether one is coding a new application or pondering the wisdom hidden in a cup of tea, Emacs can offer a process-oriented, flexible, and empowering environment that fosters creativity, productivity, and continued growth. Embracing its power can lead not only to elevated efficiency in one's work but also to deeper insights in personal and mystical practice, such as tasseography. Thus, as you delve into the captivating synthesis of Emacs and tea leaf reading, appreciate how this remarkable tool can enhance both your technical pursuits and your journey into the mystical realms of fortune-telling.

3.2. Navigating the Interface

Navigating the Emacs interface is essential for users looking to harness its capabilities effectively, especially those venturing into the realm of tea leaf reading through this powerful tool. At its core, Emacs combines simplicity and complexity, allowing users to perform both basic and advanced tasks seamlessly. Understanding how to navigate this multifaceted environment will enhance the efficiency of your readings and ensure a smooth experience as you blend the art of tasseography with digital resources.

When first opening Emacs, newcomers are greeted with a stark but functional text interface. The absence of a cluttered graphical user interface often overwhelms beginners, but it is essential to keep in mind that there lies a wealth of functionality behind the simplicity. Emacs is organized around a combination of buffers, windows, and commands, which may feel unusual at first but soon reveal an impressive level of power and flexibility.

The fundamental unit of interaction in Emacs is the buffer. A buffer serves as a space to display and edit text, and multiple buffers can be open simultaneously, allowing users to work on different documents or projects without interruption. To navigate between buffers, users can invoke the command C-x b, where C represents the Control key. This command prompts Emacs to display a list of active buffers, and users can either type the name of the buffer they wish to switch to or scroll through the list using arrow keys.

Windows, on the other hand, refer to the visible portions of the Emacs frame. A frame is the top-level container and can host multiple windows displaying different buffers. The arrangement of windows allows users to view multiple documents at once, facilitating comparisons and multitasking. To split the current window horizontally or vertically, users can employ the commands C-x 2 (for horizontal) and C-x 3 (for vertical). The division of windows is particularly useful for readers who might want to reference notes or other resources while engaging in their tea leaf interpretations.

Emacs uses keyboard shortcuts extensively, presenting a learning curve for those accustomed to mouse-centric applications. Nevertheless, mastery of these shortcuts greatly enhances productivity. For instance, the C-g command is often used to cancel an active command or to exit prompts, while C-s initiates an incremental search for text within the current buffer. Gaining familiarity with these shortcuts transforms your interaction with Emacs into a more fluid experience, allowing you to focus on your readings rather than the mechanics of navigation.

One of the standout features of Emacs is its ability to be customized and extended through its built-in scripting language, Emacs Lisp (Elisp). Users can create their own functions, key bindings, and even entire modes tailored to their unique needs. This customization is achieved through the init.el or .emacs configuration files, where users can script various enhancements. When embarking on your tea leaf reading journey, consider developing specific functions within Emacs that streamline your process—such as automatically categorizing symbols or recording interpretations. As you grow more accustomed to the interface, your ability to tailor these functions will deepen, allowing for a reflection of your personal reading style.

External packages also significantly enhance Emacs' functionality. The MELPA repository offers a vast collection of pre-built packages that users can install to improve their experience. For instance, packages like org-mode can assist in organizing your tea readings, creating structured notes, and journaling insights from your interpretations. Mastering package management through M-x package-install followed by the package name allows you to rapidly expand Emacs' capabilities. The ability to curate tools and resources that resonate with your reading journey reflects the true strength of Emacs' community-driven infrastructure.

Moreover, navigating the interface also involves learning about modes—specific configurations that Emacs applies to buffers catering to different tasks. Major modes dictate programming language syntax and auto-completion features, while minor modes offer supplementary functionalities such as spell-checking or visual aids. Identifying and utilizing appropriate modes for your reading might include text modes enriched with features for documentation and analysis. For instance, activating text-mode when recording your readings can ensure that you have access to formatting options that create clarity and organization.

As you delve into tea leaf reading through Emacs, integrating mindfulness practices into your navigation can foster a more profound connection with your interpretations. Before starting, consider setting an intention or focusing your thoughts through meditation; this mental preparation can enhance your engagement with the Emacs interface as you transition into a reflective state fitting for divination.

In conclusion, navigating the Emacs interface opens up a world of possibilities that merge seamlessly with the mystical practice of tea leaf reading. By mastering the basic features, familiarizing yourself with keyboard shortcuts, and embracing customization, you lay the groundwork for a transformative experience. Each interaction within Emacs not only sets the stage for insightful readings but also fosters a creative space where tradition meets modernity. As you continue to explore the integration of Emacs into your tasseography practices, remember that the interface is a living entity—one that adapts to your journey, encouraging exploration, growth, and discovery every step of the way.

3.3. Customization and Extensions

Customization and extensions are at the heart of the Emacs experience, allowing users to tailor their environment in ways that enhance both productivity and enjoyment. For readers seeking to practice tasseography through Emacs, the process of customization weaves in with the overall aim of enhancing the reading experience, leveraging Emacs' robust capabilities to create a personalized and effective toolkit for divination.

One of the initial steps in customizing Emacs involves modifying the configuration file, typically named .emacs or init.el. This file serves as a canvas on which users can write scripts in Emacs Lisp to adjust functionalities or settings that suit their workflow. Such customization can manifest in various ways, from altering the appearance—such as themes, font styles, and colors that reflect the user's personality and preferences—to optimizing keybindings that streamline tasks relevant to tea leaf readings. For example, users may find it beneficial to create custom keybindings for commonly used commands specific to tasseography, allowing them to switch quickly between buffer windows for documenting notes or referencing symbolic libraries with ease.

Emacs boasts a powerful extension ecosystem, primarily accessed through package managers like MELPA (Milkypostman's Emacs Lisp Package Archive). This repository offers a treasure trove of packages that can expand Emacs' functionalities. For instance, users interested in enhancing their reading process with digital tools can rely on packages like org-mode, an incredibly versatile system used for organizing notes and managing tasks. In the context of tasseography, users could create organized notes that encapsulate their tea leaf readings, interpretations, and personal reflections. By integrating features such as task lists and calendar synchronization, Emacs becomes a central hub for merging ritualistic practices with structured documentation.

Beyond organizational tools, there are packages specifically designed for text analysis and natural language processing, which could support users in interpreting symbols and making connections to larger themes within their readings. For example, employing a package that analyzes common phrases or patterns in journal entries can allow readers to develop insights over time, tracing the evolution of personal symbolism and the nuances of their interpretations.

In addition to these, users can design custom symbol libraries within Emacs tailored to their unique interpretations derived from tea leaf reading. A dedicated space for symbols allows for quick reference, and users might find it beneficial to add descriptions or context alongside visual representations of the symbols. With a few lines of code, a dedicated function can be created to display relevant information about a particular symbol that appears during a reading, enhancing comprehension and connection with the practice.

But customization can extend beyond just functionality—users can enrich their Emacs experience aesthetically as well. By selecting themes that evoke tranquility or inspiration, readers can create an inviting atmosphere as they engage with their readings. The ability to embed images or illustrations of various symbols directly within Emacs can also bring an interactive aspect to the practice. Integrating visual elements enhances the reading experience, reinforcing the symbolic meanings tied to the actual shapes of the leaves left in the cup.

The Emacs community is also an invaluable resource. Engaging with fellow users through forums, chat channels, and local meetups can foster the exchange of ideas and further enhance one's environment. Many members are willing to share their configurations or even extend their codes for others to customize. While the world of tea leaf reading may seem niche, incorporating themes and discussions around the practice with those who enjoy programming opens new pathways for innovation and creativity.

Moreover, as technology advances, the prospect of integrating modern tools into traditional practices remains ripe with potential. Users may explore connecting Emacs to online platforms for collaborative readings or integrating artificial intelligence to assist with symbol recognition, potentially unearthing new interpretations previously unexplored.

The customizability of Emacs fosters an environment of continuous learning and growth, with every reader able to adapt their toolkit as they advance in their practice. Regardless of how one chooses to personalize their Emacs setup for tea leaf reading, the ultimate goal remains—to cultivate an enriching experience that blends ancient traditions with modern enhancements while encouraging personal expression.

To summarize, the power of customization and extension within Emacs lies not solely in technical prowess but in the opportunity it presents for users to shape their tools according to individual needs and creative inclinations. By combining thoughtful configurations, a supportive community, and a willingness to explore new integrations, readers can transform their Emacs environment into a vibrant space conducive to both reflection and the mystical practices of tasseography. This melding of the old and the new not only honors the roots of tea leaf reading but also paves the way for a novel journey enriched through the wonders of technology.

3.4. Adapting Emacs for Non-Programming Uses

Tapping into the potential of Emacs for non-programming uses can transform it from a mere text editor into a versatile tool that enhances various aspects of everyday life, including personal development, creative expression, and ritualistic practices like tea leaf reading. In this context, Emacs serves not only as a space for writing lines of code but also as a digital sanctuary where one can engage in reflective practices, organize thoughts, and cultivate a deeper understanding of oneself and the world around.

At its foundation, Emacs offers a minimalist interface, encouraging users to focus on their tasks without unnecessary distractions. This aspect is particularly beneficial for practices that demand mental clarity and concentration, such as tea leaf reading. The ability to document thoughts and insights instantly in a structured manner can help deepen your understanding of the messages conveyed through tea leaves. Using Emacs' simple text buffers, readers can maintain logs of their readings, recording interpretations and reflections over time. This not only aligns with practices of mindfulness but also creates a tangible record that can be revisited, offering perspective on the subtleties of personal growth and evolution.

Emacs' flexibility is one of its most compelling features. Users can customize the interface, adjust keybindings, and even integrate various packages to suit their unique approaches. For instance, a practitioner might choose to tailor their environment for tea readings by creating specific commands that assist in maintaining a log of symbols, patterns, and interpretations. Creating an Emacs configuration that includes a dedicated space for logging tea leaf readings can streamline the documentation process, allowing for greater focus on the ritual and exploration of meaning rather than the logistics of record-keeping.

For those who engage in the artistic or intuitive aspects of life, Emacs serves as a blank canvas where creativity can flourish. The editor's simplicity allows for artistic expression through writing poetry, journaling thoughts, or sketching out ideas related to clairvoyance without the confines of structured programming language. In this regard, using Emacs for creative exercises or to document reflections on the tea leaf reading experience opens new channels for self-expression and insight that extend beyond the mere divinatory act.

Moreover, organizations are key to enriching the tea leaf reading practice. Emacs can effectively manage notes taken after readings, enabling users to categorize insights based on recurring symbols or themes encountered in their journeys. By employing tools within Emacs, such as Org mode, practitioners can create a well-structured system for organizing their notes — setting up templates for readings, categorizing symbols, and maintaining a repository of interpretations that can be referenced later. This method allows individuals to track their development over time, build a personal lexicon of symbols, and create pathways for introspection that guide future readings.

The collaborative potential of Emacs opens further possibilities for community engagement in non-coding contexts. By connecting with fellow practitioners — whether online or in-person through work-shops — users can exchange insights, share configurations, or even develop joint projects that blend technology with the traditional practices of tasseography. Emacs becomes a collaborative platform where ideas can be discussed, research can be conducted, and shared experiences can lead to profound learnings about interpretations and personal pathways.

In a world increasingly dominated by distractions, Emacs provides an environment that encourages deep work and attentiveness. This focus promotes mindfulness practices tied to tea leaf reading, enhancing the communion between practitioner and ritual. Emacs can assist in creating a meditative space where individuals reflect and engage more profoundly with their practices, enriching the overall experience and fostering a sense of peace and clarity.

As new tools and technologies emerge, adapting Emacs for non-pro-gramming uses — especially in the realm of intuitive practices such as tea leaf reading — highlights the blend of tradition and innovation within personal and spiritual growth. It empowers users to engage deeply with their readings, document experiences, share insights, and cultivate an enriched understanding of themselves and their journeys. This evolution of Emacs as a multifunctional tool embodies the spirit of blending ancient methods with modern capabilities, making the art of tasseography both accessible and deeply personal for practitioners in a digital world.

3.5. Community and Resources

In the realm of tea leaf reading and tasseography, community and resources play pivotal roles in enriching the practice and expanding personal understanding. The melding of ancient traditions with modern technology, particularly through platforms like Emacs, creates opportunities not only for introspective readings but also for collective learning and sharing. Engaging with a community of fellow practitioners opens pathways for insight, connection, and growth.

The Emacs user community thrives on collaboration and the sharing of knowledge, fostering an environment that allows both seasoned users and newcomers to learn from one another. As tea leaf reading embraces digital tools, practitioners can harness the power of this community to share their readings, techniques, and interpretations of symbols. Online forums, social media groups, and wikis dedicated to Emacs users provide a wealth of resources, including tutorials, configuration suggestions, and thematic discussions centered on the blend of coding and divination practices. By participating in these discussions, readers can refine their methodologies, explore varying perspectives on interpretations, and exchange creative approaches that other practitioners have found successful.

For those new to both Emacs and tasseography, discovering a supportive community is invaluable. Learning the intricacies of Emacs can initially be overwhelming—its complexity is balanced by its adaptability, making peer support essential. Many users share configuration files, known as dotfiles, which can provide templates and scaffolding for those looking to tailor their Emacs environment for tea leaf readings specifically. Engaging in Q&A threads or dedicated community discussions can guide users through the learning curve, encouraging exploration and experimentation in a non-judgmental space.

Furthermore, community-led workshops and meetups are golden opportunities for practitioners to deepen their understanding of tasseography while honing their skills in Emacs. These gatherings promote hands-on experiences, where participants can practice readings together, experience different interpretative styles, and engage in discussions about the meanings of various symbols. In such environments, readers can amplify the study of tea leaves, learning not just through solitary practice but also from the shared wisdom of others. Collaborative readings are especially impactful; they can lead to collective insights that might not emerge in individual explorations.

Beyond interpersonal connection, numerous resources are available that cater specifically to integrating Emacs with tasseography. Mitigating the complexity of the coding and customization process, tutorial videos and written guides provide step-by-step instructions on setting up Emacs to log readings, record notes, and manage data related to tea leaves. These documents serve as a bridge for those transitioning from traditional methods to a more structured, digital approach to their divination practices. Additionally, dedicated blogs and websites often explore how to leverage Emacs' features, such as Org mode, to maintain structured journals for documenting tea leaf interpretations effectively.

Conversations around tea leaf reading may also emerge in larger online forums dedicated to broader spiritual or metaphysical topics, where users share their experiences and challenges in both reading and interpreting tea leaves. These platforms can become a repository for shared techniques, symbol dictionaries, and research that expands the community's collective knowledge. By pooling resources, members bolster their understanding, minimizing the challenges that may inhibit personal growth or comprehension of the practice.

Embracing the diverse strands of information available allows practitioners to dive more deeply into the art of tasseography. Whether seeking out podcasts discussing the nuances of tea divination, reading literature on historical interpretations of symbols, or following social media profiles dedicated to tea leaf readings, community resources contribute to a well-rounded approach to understanding this ancient practice. With today's technology interlinked with these age-old traditions, the flexibility and creative approaches community engagement offers can only enhance your tea leaf reading experience.

In conclusion, the interplay between community and resources embodies the spirit of collaboration and growth within the tea leaf reading practice. Both Emacs users and tasseography enthusiasts can find shared perspectives, encouragement, and guidance as they delve into the mystique of tea leaves. Invoking tradition while embracing modernity unveils a vibrant landscape for personal exploration, creativity, and connection. This symbiotic relationship underscores the importance of community—an ever-expanding framework that weaves together the past, present, and future of tasseography in an increasingly interconnected world. As you embark on your journey through tea leaf reading, may you embrace the resources and connections that abound, guiding you toward deeper insights and enriching experiences in this captivating art.

4. The Fusion of Tasseography and Technology

4.1. Tasseography in the Digital Age

The digital age has ushered in a transformation in the way we engage with traditional practices, including the ancient art of tasseography, or tea leaf reading. This merging of the mystical with modern technology has captivated a new generation of practitioners, allowing them to explore the depths of tea leaves in ways that were previously unimaginable. The tactile experience of reading tea leaves now intertwines with the analytical and organizational power that tools like Emacs provide.

Tasseography, at its core, is the practice of interpreting patterns formed by tea leaves remaining in a cup after consumption. Traditionally, these readings were intimate affairs involving personal insights, future predictions, and explorations into one's internal landscape. With the rise of digital tools, however, this ancient practice has begun to adapt, incorporate new techniques, and broaden its accessibility. As tea leaf readings become more intertwined with technology, we can see how the digital landscape innovate the way we interpret signs, structure insights, and engage with the metaphysical.

The integration of Emacs, a customizable and extensible text editor, with tasseography can enhance the way practitioners interact with their readings. Emacs offers a platform for managing notes, documenting readings, and analyzing the patterns that emerge from tea leaves, all within a single interface. The ability to customize keybindings and scripts in Emacs allows users to create an environment tailored for tea leaf reading—turning tea into a canvas for artistic exploration mixed with the precision of programming.

As practitioners sip their warm cups, they can document their experiences in real-time, utilizing Emacs to catalog symbols that appear during their readings. The possibility of developing a personal symbol dictionary or creating templates for recording insights complements the reflective aspect of tasseography. No longer bound to paper and pens, readers can explore the layers of meaning in digital form, curating their journeys through unique interpretations.

Moreover, with the vast repository of resources available online, practitioners can enrich their readings by connecting with others in the community. Online forums, social media groups, and dedicated platforms for Emacs users promote sharing of readings, symbols, and personal interpretations. This communal approach not only democratizes the practice of tasseography but also enhances individual learning. Engaging with others brings diverse perspectives and encourages the exploration of different techniques—resulting in an enriched understanding of symbols and their meanings beyond the confines of a solitary interpretation.

In addition to community engagement, the use of technology allows for a comprehensive approach to readings. Digital tools can help document patterns over time, creating a repository rich with personal history—where readers can trace their growth and changing interpretations influenced by life experiences. For instance, by maintaining a digital journal using Emacs, practitioners can reflect on their evolving interpretations, make connections between various symbols, and enhance their intuition in the reading process.

Another fascinating point lies in the advancements in AI and machine learning. While it may seem worlds apart from the intuitive practice of divination, these technologies could be harnessed to analyze patterns in readings, offering insights based on historical interpretations and common symbols drawn from extensive databases. Imagine an Emacs setup that incorporates tools to recognize frequently encountered shapes, providing users guidance based purely on algorithmic results while still allowing space for personal reflection and intuitive guidance.

Furthermore, the accessibility provided by technology enables the dissemination of tasseography to broader audiences. Digital platforms can foster tutorials, readings, and accessible resources for novices who may be intrigued by the practice but unsure where to begin. This outreach transforms traditional tea leaf reading from a niche skill to an engaging practice open to many.

The merging of tasseography with digital tools like Emacs doesn't come without challenges. There will always be debates regarding the authenticity of traditional practices versus modern interpretations. Navigating the dynamics of balancing established rituals with evolving methodologies requires a thoughtful approach, sensitive to the historical significance of tea leaf reading and the innovative spirit that drives modern practices.

In essence, the fusion of tasseography and technology invites practitioners into a dynamic new era, where exploration, creativity, and community thrive. By embracing the analytical prowess of digital tools alongside the ancient wisdom carried by tea leaves, individuals can cultivate deeper insights both personally and collectively. As we continue to explore this captivating synthesis, tea leaf reading in the digital age not only honors the past but also ignites new pathways for understanding ourselves and our journey through life. This interplay between tradition and technology offers a reflective tapestry that allows us to unveil the potential of our experiences through the art of tasseography.

4.2. Integrating Emacs with Tasseography

Integrating Emacs with the art of tasseography offers a powerful platform that merges the intuitive practice of tea leaf reading with the structured, versatile capabilities of this sophisticated text editor. This integration not only enhances the efficiency of readings but also infuses the experience with an element of technological creativity. By employing Emacs, practitioners can broaden their perspective on interpreting tea leaves and deepen their connections to their readings.

One of the most compelling ways to incorporate Emacs into the practice of tasseography is through the customization of your reading environment. Through the use of initial configuration files like .emacs or init.el, users can set up specific modes and keybindings that cater to their tea leaf reading needs. For instance, a dedicated mode can be created within Emacs to simulate a digital tea leaf journal, allowing users to log their readings seamlessly while incorporating elements such as timestamping and categorization by symbol.

The concept of documenting readings digitally can further be enhanced by establishing a structured template in which practitioners can enter details related to each reading, such as the type of tea used, the symbols identified, and their respective meanings. This framework not only aids in maintaining organization but also facilitates the analysis of patterns over time. By revisiting their readings, users may discover recurring themes or insights, informing their understanding of their personal journey and further enriching their interaction with tea leaves.

Moreover, utilizing Emacs' powerful text manipulation capabilities can aid in the development of a personalized symbol dictionary. Users can create a comprehensive list of tea leaf symbols, integrating interpretations and associated personal insights into a single document. This symbol library can be referenced at any time during readings, ensuring that readers have access to resources that foster greater clarity in interpretation. The ability to search for specific symbols quickly enhances the flow of readings and allows for a more engaging process.

In addition to logging and documentation, the integration of tools like Org mode can revolutionize how users approach their tasseography practice. Through Org mode, readers can structure their tea leaves readings in a hierarchical format, creating interconnected documents that maintain a robust reference guide. This organization brings to life the connections between various readings, helping users to visualize how their interpretations evolve and relate back to their personal narrative or experiences.

Furthermore, the technological fusion with Emacs invites community engagement through online forums and digital sharing platforms. Practitioners can share their personalized Emacs configurations, symbol libraries, and unique interpretations with others in the tea leaf reading community. Engaging with fellow enthusiasts online fosters a sense of connection and shared learning, dispelling the notion of tasseography as a solitary endeavor.

To enhance further the integration of Emacs in tasseography, practitioners can also turn to programming aspects of the text editor. Writing scripts in Emacs Lisp (Elisp) to automate certain tasks—like generating random tea leaf patterns for interpretation can add a playful element to the readings. This innovation encourages experimentation, inviting users to explore various interpretations through an interactive medium, which can, in turn, lead to deeper insights.

In this age of rapid technological advancement, maintaining a balance between tradition and innovation remains a core principle. While technology is woven into the tapestry of modern reading practices, the inherent spirit of tasseography should always be honored. Encouraging a respectful dialogue between old and new—through the use of software like Emacs—adds layers of depth to the experience, enhancing both intuitive and analytical aspects of reading tea leaves.

In summary, combining Emacs with tasseography creates a unique framework that elevates the experience of reading tea leaves. By harnessing customization and community engagement, readers can document their journeys, learn from one another, and explore the evolving meanings of tea leaves within their own lives. This integration does not merely serve as a digital enhancement but embraces the rich tradition of tasseography, inviting both innovation and respect for its historical roots. The synergy between Emacs and tea leaf reading truly invites practitioners to engage more profoundly with the symbols and stories that emerge from that mystical cup of tea, propelling them toward greater understanding and insight.

4.3. Developing a Tasseography Emacs Setup

In the world of Emacs, setting up a customized environment tailored for tasseography can significantly enhance both the efficiency and depth of your tea leaf reading experience. The following guide outlines the key steps to developing a comprehensive Emacs setup that caters specifically to the mystical art of interpreting tea leaves while incorporating the advanced features of Emacs.

To begin with, establishing your workspace involves creating a dedicated environment within Emacs where you can easily document, analyze, and reflect upon your readings. The first step is to identify a suitable configuration file, typically named init.el or .emacs, where you will script your personalized setup. This file acts as the backbone for enabling various functionalities tailored for tasseography.

1. Setting Up the Basic Environment: Open your configuration file and start by setting basic settings that will make your workspace more comfortable. Adjust font sizes, colors, and themes to create a soothing visual experience conducive to meditation and introspection during tea readings. You can apply a calming color scheme by including themes that resonate with relaxed and natural aesthetics.

2. Custom Commands for Documenting Readings: Creating specific functions or commands within Emacs can aid in documenting your readings swiftly. For example, coding a simple command to open a new buffer with a predefined template for logging readings might involve defining key bindings that allow you to launch this template effortlessly. Below is a basic example of how you might set this up:

```
(defun create-reading-log ()
  "Create a new buffer for tea leaf reading logs."
  (interactive)
  (switch-to-buffer "*Tea Reading Log*")
  (insert "Date: " (format-time-string "%Y-%m-%d") "\n")
  (insert "Type of Tea: \n")
  (insert "Symbols Interpreted: \n")
  (insert "Reflections: \n\n")
  (goto-char (point-min))
  (text-mode))
(global-set-key (kbd "C-c r") 'create-reading-log)
```

With this function, you can quickly create a reading log each time you wish to record insights from your tea leaf readings.

3. Integration with Org Mode: One of Emacs' most powerful features is Org Mode, which allows for structured note-taking and organization. Implementing Org Mode for tea leaf readings can transform the way you document and analyze your sessions. You can create an Org file dedicated to tea readings and establish a hierarchical structure to categorize symbols, insights, and personal reflections.

   For example, set up categories such as:
   - Readings by Date
   - Symbol Interpretations
   - Themes and Patterns
   - Personal Insights

By utilizing Org Mode's rich feature set, you can integrate tasks, schedules, and links, enabling a comprehensive overview of your tea leaf journey.

4. Custom Symbol Library: Compile a personalized library of symbols associated with tea leaves. You can create a dedicated buffer or Org file that comprises all the symbols you encounter, alongside their meanings and interpretations. This bibliographic resource can be indispensable during readings as you reference it quickly. For efficiency, consider writing a function that allows you to search through this symbol library using keywords.

5. Visual Aids: Since Emacs supports text-based illustrations, consider including ASCII art or simple sketches of common symbols, which could provide visual reference during your readings. Use Emacs' capabilities to embed images that represent specific symbols within your documentation.

6. Automating Reflections: Write scripts that allow you to reflect on past readings by displaying previous logs and encouraging you to document changes in interpretations over time. This reflective practice not only opens a dialogue with your inner self but also nurtures a deeper connection with the symbolic meanings of tea leaves.

7. Community and Resource Sharing: Engage with digital platforms where Emacs users gather. Participate in forums and discussion threads dedicated to tea leaf reading to share configurations, exchange ideas, and gather tips from others who have successfully integrated their practices with Emacs. You can even create a public repository of your Emacs setup for others interested in tasseography to explore and use as a starting point.

8. Maintaining Mindfulness in Practice: Emacs can serve as your mindful digital space. As you prepare to read tea leaves, utilize functions in Emacs that center your thoughts, such as a meditation timer or prompts encouraging reflections before beginning your reading sessions.

9. Experiment and Evolve: Embrace the iterative nature of personalization. Explore different packages within Emacs that might enhance your setup, such as those focused on journaling or visualization tools. Feel free to iterate on your configuration as you grow in your practice and discover what works best for you.

10. Reflective Closure: After each reading session, include space in your logs for reflections on the reading process itself. What did you notice during the interpretation? How did the symbols resonate with your current life? This practice of reflecting not just on the symbols but on the act of reading itself can enhance your growth as a reader.

By harnessing the power of Emacs to create a tailored environment for tasseography, you set the stage for a rich and rewarding experience that combines ancient wisdom with modern technology. Not only do you facilitate organization and analysis, but you also open yourself to a deeper engagement with the intuitive aspects of tea leaf reading. Through this integrated approach, your adventures in tasseography can blossom into profound journeys of self-discovery and insight.

4.4. Case Studies: Success Stories

In the enchanting realm of tasseography, countless practitioners have embraced the fusion of ancient wisdom and modern technology, finding inventive ways to enhance their tea leaf reading journeys through the power of Emacs. Each story reflects not just personal growth but illustrates the transformative potential of integrating traditional divinatory practices with sophisticated digital tools. This section delves into several inspiring case studies that showcase the success stories of individuals who have skillfully navigated this confluence of tradition and technology.

One notable example is that of Sarah, a software engineer who, after years of dabbling in tea leaf reading, sought to deepen her practice through the structured and customizable environment offered by Emacs. Initially intimidated by the interface, Sarah began with the basics: journaling her readings in a simple text format. As her comfort with Emacs grew, she discovered the incredible versatility of Org mode, which allowed her to categorize her readings, create links between symbols, and review her interpretations systematically. Sarah developed a system where she could easily input new readings, associate them with specific teas, and seamlessly reflect on the patterns that emerged over time. The real breakthrough came when she devised a personal dictionary of tea leaf symbols, complete with visual references and interpretations. This ongoing project within Emacs not only enhanced her personal practice but also served as a valuable resource for sharing insights with a burgeoning online community dedicated to tasseography.

Meanwhile, across the globe, James, an educator and mindfulness coach, stumbled upon the idea of using Emacs to facilitate community workshops focused on tea leaf reading. By designing an interactive platform where participants could log their readings collaboratively, James created a digital space that encouraged participants to share their experiences and insights. He used Emacs to document workshop materials, and along with participants, they created a collective reading log, allowing everyone to reflect on their journeys. The feedback from the workshops highlighted the participants' enjoyment in having a shared repository of readings, fostering connections amongst each other and empowering individuals to explore their interpretations more boldly. The communal aspect—that merging of personal journeys through a collective lens—allowed for deeper engagement and growth.

In a more creative endeavor, Mia, an artist and writer, sought to blend her passions for art and tea leaf reading through her Emacs setup. Mia configured her environment to include sections dedicated to both journaling her readings and sketching interpretations based on what she discerned from the leaves. Using a tablet and digitizing her art, she incorporated her sketches into her Emacs documents, creating a visually striking narrative of her tea leaf experiences. This artistic integration transformed her readings into compelling storytelling, lifting her practice beyond traditional boundaries. By sharing her work in various art forums and Emacs communities, Mia inspired others to consider incorporating creativity into their own readings, thus fostering a holistic approach to tasseography.

As Emacs users continue to explore innovative pathways for tea leaf reading, Clara's story emerges as an example of adaptability. A consultant who frequently travels for work, Clara felt disconnected from her tea leaf reading practice as her schedule became increasingly hectic. Looking for a solution, she set up Emacs on her laptop and utilized cloud syncing to access her notes on the go. She streamlined her workflow by employing shortcuts to quickly log readings and reflections, using snippets of time during her travels to maintain her practice. The ability to document her tea leaf readings regardless of location not only kept her engaged with her intuitive practice but also highlighted Emacs' adaptability to modern lifestyles. Clara's success story exemplifies how individuals can maintain continuity in personal practices even amid the chaos of daily life.

Lastly, we encounter Oliver, a digital humanities scholar, who worked with an interdisciplinary team to develop a research project that combined Emacs with tea leaf reading's historical contexts. By documenting historical interpretations of symbols and their values across cultures, they built a digital archive accessible via Emacs, formatted for academic use. This project not only enriched their understanding but encouraged collaboration among fellow scholars intrigued by the intersection of tradition and modern interpretations. Oliver's interdisciplinary endeavor illuminated the potential for Emacs to serve as a repository of knowledge, encapsulating a wealth of findings that contribute to the scholarly conversation surrounding tasseography.

Across these diverse narratives, the unifying theme of success in integrating Emacs into the practice of tasseography emerges clear: practitioners have embraced the opportunity to enhance their readings through organization, community engagement, artistic exploration, adaptability, and academic contributions. Each success story illustrates a remarkable journey towards weaving together the past and present, inspiring a new generation to explore the profound insights that can be revealed through the humble tea leaves. As practitioners continue to refine their methods and adapt to evolving technologies, the future of tasseography remains vibrant, promising a wealth of new interpretations and collective discoveries. Through these cases, one can recognize that success in tasseography is as much about personal insight as it is about collaboration, creativity, and critical engagement with both tradition and modernity.

4.5. Future Prospects in Tasseography

The future of tasseography, particularly when intertwined with advancements in technology, offers a vibrant landscape rich with potential for practitioners. As the traditional art of tea leaf reading evolves to meet contemporary needs, several exciting prospects present themselves, inviting both innovation and deeper understanding. We can anticipate a variety of trends fueled by technology, community interactions, and changing societal values, all of which will contribute to the practice's growth and accessibility.

One of the most profound changes on the horizon is the increasing adoption of digital tools to facilitate the tea leaf reading process. With platforms like Emacs providing a flexible and customizable framework, practitioners can now document their readings more systematically than ever before. This evolution not only encourages the maintenance of logs and reflections but also empowers readers to analyze patterns and recurring symbols over time. Future enhancements could include advanced data visualization tools within Emacs that would allow users to intuitively map their interpretations, correlating life events with specific readings and insights derived from their experiences.

As we navigate this digital age, the fusion of artificial intelligence with tasseography becomes an intriguing possibility. Imagine an AI-driven feature that recognizes common shapes and suggests potential interpretations based on vast databases of historical readings. Such tools could serve not only as valuable companions to seasoned readers but also as entry points for newcomers, easing their introduction to the nuances of tea leaf reading. This integration can help demystify symbols and render them more relatable, reinforcing the practice's accessibility.

Moreover, the global exchange of ideas and cultures heralds a new era of collaboration among practitioners from different backgrounds. With online forums and social media groups flourishing, tea leaf readers can now share insights, techniques, and experiences at an unprecedented scale. This communal aspect will likely contribute to the evolution of new interpretative styles, blending traditional frameworks with contemporary interpretations. A cross-cultural dialogue can enrich the practice, bringing fresh symbols and meanings into the collective lexicon of tasseography, while also honoring its historical roots.

The rise of wellness culture and the increasing emphasis on holistic approaches to self-discovery will further shape the future of tasseography. People are increasingly seeking practices that connect them to their inner selves, and tea leaf reading provides a unique avenue for this exploration. As the practice continues to evolve, it will likely be embraced within therapeutic contexts—encouraging individuals to engage in mindfulness, introspection, and self-reflection. Combining these elements with digital platforms will foster environments where readers can not only interpret symbols but also cultivate personal narratives that resonate with their lived experiences.

We will also see a more pronounced focus on the ethical dimensions of tea leaf reading in the coming years. As the practice becomes more integrated into personal coaching and community support frameworks, ethical considerations will arise regarding the responsibilities of readers toward their clients. Establishing clear guidelines and encouraging transparent practices in interpretation will foster a sense of trust and integrity within the community. This shift will likely empower practitioners to engage more thoughtfully with their readings and the impact they have on others' lives.

In terms of education and learning, there is a growing potential for formalized training programs that help readers hone their skills, understand the historical contexts of symbols, and teach effective techniques for interpretation. Whether through online courses, workshops, or community programs, this push toward education can further professionalize the practice and elevate its esteem as a respected method of divination and personal exploration.

Looking ahead, as technology progresses, we can expect to see advancements in how tea leaves are prepared and consumed, potentially influencing their symbolic meanings. New methods of brewing or unique blends of tea used in readings may contribute fresh interpretations to the practice. Such changes will provide ongoing opportunities for innovation, inviting readers to explore how variations in tea can amplify or shift the messages conveyed through their leaf patterns.

Ultimately, the future prospects of tasseography are bright and full of opportunity. The practice's adaptability, when combined with technology and community engagement, will allow it to flourish in various forms. Bridge-building between tradition and innovation paves the way for new interpretations rich in meaning while ensuring the core of tea leaf reading—the pursuit of personal insight—remains accessible for generations to come.

As we embrace these potential advancements, it is vital for practitioners to remain curious, open-minded, and engaged in the evolving landscape of tasseography. By balancing the roots of tradition with the excitement of innovation, individuals can cultivate profound practices that not only reveal the narratives of their tea leaves but also connect them with larger themes of existence, identity, and communal cooperation. The journey ahead beckons: a unique path await for those willing to unravel the mysteries encoded in tea leaves while leveraging the treasures of modernity.

5. Understanding Tea Leaves: The Basics

5.1. Types of Tea Leaves and Their Significance

In the exploration of tea leaf reading, the types of tea leaves used in tasseography bear significant meaning and influence the overall interpretation and experience of each reading. Various tea leaves not only differ in taste and aroma but also symbolize unique qualities that can inform the reader's understanding of the patterns formed by the leaves.

The most common types of tea used in readings include green tea, black tea, white tea, oolong tea, and herbal blends. Each of these possesses distinct properties and historical associations that enhance the nuances in interpretations.

Green tea is often regarded as a symbol of renewal and vitality. The fresh, earthy flavor and delicate nature of green tea evoke feelings of clarity, balance, and rejuvenation. When leaves of green tea are interpreted, they may signal new beginnings or a reawakening in the querent's life. This type of tea tends to foster an environment of mindfulness, prompting reflections on personal growth and self-discovery. Readings involving green tea may generally emphasize intuition and the importance of being present within one's circumstances.

On the other hand, black tea is commonly associated with strength, grounding, and stability. Its bold flavor and robust character connotate resilience, making it ideal for readings focused on life challenges or decision-making. The interpretations of symbols formed by black tea leaves often reveal obstacles, necessitating perseverance and determination. The darker tones of black tea can also symbolize the unknown, urging readers to confront their fears or uncertainties with courage.

White tea, with its subtle elegance and lightness, symbolizes purity, simplicity, and enlightenment. It is a choice tea for those seeking clarity in their readings. The interpretations derived from white tea leaves can often lean towards themes of innocence, transparency, and the unveiling of truths. This tea encourages honesty and authenticity

—qualities that resonate deeply with both the reader and the person seeking insight. When white tea leaves are present in a reading, it may indicate that the querent is experiencing or requires a moment of clarity.

Oolong tea presents a fascinating case in tasseography, symbolizing transitions and balance between opposites. This partially fermented tea holds unique properties that foster creativity and spontaneity. Individuals engaging in readings with oolong tea may be encouraged to embrace change and the fluid nature of life. The patterns left by oolong tea leaves often underscore the significance of adaptability, suggesting that the querent may need to navigate opposing forces within their experiences as they seek resolution or clarity.

Herbal teas encompass a wide range of ingredients and can bring a diverse set of meanings to tea leaf readings. Depending on the specific herbs present, herbal teas can embody themes of healing, protection, or transformation. For example, chamomile known for its calming properties may suggest the need for relaxation and several positive outcomes in stressful situations. In contrast, peppermint tea could herald a strong sense of determination and directness, possibly indicating swift changes on the horizon. Practitioners must be savvy in their interpretations of herbal blends since these teas often reflect broader emotional or physical states that can deeply inform readings.

When readers engage with the intricacies of the types of tea leaves, they must consider the distinct cultures and histories surrounding each tea. The variations in preparation, serving styles, and social traditions often impact the resonance of meanings drawn from the leaves. Practitioners may also choose to investigate the unique agricultural backgrounds or brewing methods that could further illuminate their readings.

As you navigate the world of tea leaf reading, it is essential to recognize that the choice of tea leaves extends beyond personal preference; it invites a deeper exploration into the narrative your readings create. Each tea type reveals a layer of context and complexity, enriching the practice while imbuing it with historical significance and cultural diversity. By understanding and appreciating the significance of different tea leaves, practitioners can refine their interpretations, ultimately enhancing the insight gained through this enchanting art.

The delicate interplay between the chosen tea leaves and their symbolic meanings not only heightens the effectiveness of the reading but also enhances the experience as practitioners tune in to the messages carried through time and tradition, allowing the leaves to tell their own stories in conjunction with the reader's intuitive journey.

5.2. Interpreting Shapes and Patterns

Interpreting shapes and patterns formed by tea leaves is a pivotal aspect of tasseography, allowing practitioners to unlock the narratives hidden within their cups. The intricacies involved in understanding these symbols help readers connect the visual impressions created by the leaves to personal insights, life situations, and future possibilities. Mastering the art of interpretation transforms tea leaf reading from a mere pastime into a profound tool for self-discovery and reflection.

The interpretation process begins immediately after the cup is turned upside down, allowing the remaining tea leaves to settle into unique shapes and patterns. These formations are most often examined by the reader, who must cultivate a sense of intuition and mindfulness. The symbols that emerge can lend insights about numerous aspects of life, from interpersonal relationships to career developments and personal growth. Every shape holds meaning, and the contextual understanding of these symbols makes all the difference.

To decode the meanings, readers start by observing the overall structure of the shapes created by the tea leaves. For instance, a circular formation might symbolize wholeness or completion, suggesting that a certain cycle in the reader's life has come to an end. Conversely, angular shapes may indicate conflict or abrupt changes approaching in the future. The ability to identify the emotional tone of the symbols often informs the interpretation significantly.

As the reader examines the specific individual shapes, they must also look for twists and connections between them. For example, a line connecting a heart shape to a star could represent a romantic relationship that has the potential to lead to success or enlightenment. On the contrary, if a symbol appears fractured, it may suggest rifts or difficulties coming to light. This interconnected analysis encourages readers to pay attention to the relationship between shapes—both themselves and the broader context within which they emerge.

Familiarity with common symbols enhances the understanding of their meanings. For instance, certain shapes have established interpretations within the community of tea leaf readers. A star can symbolize hope and guidance, while a crescent moon often denotes intuition and femininity. Understanding the common lexicon of symbols allows readers to speak the language of their tea leaves fluently and makes it easier to convey their insights to others.

Additionally, practitioners should hone their observational skills. Recognizing small details in the shapes, such as the density or the orientation of leaves, adds another layer of depth to interpretations. For instance, dense clusters of leaves might symbolize urgency or a merge of multiple influences converging in one aspect of the reader's life, whereas sparse leaves could represent the opposite—suggesting delays or a lack of focus.

The setting in which the interpretation occurs can also affect perceptions of the formed shapes. Mindfulness and emotional states during the reading process can color interpretations. A tranquil, relaxed setting will often evoke clearer insights, while a chaotic or distracting environment may confound the connection to the symbols formed. Therefore, practitioners should create a serene atmosphere conducive to reflection and understanding.

To cultivate interpretation skills, readers can establish a regular practice, journaling their readings and reflecting on the meanings and outcomes tied to the symbols they identify. This process enables them to track how interpretations evolve and how their intuition becomes sharper over time. Over time, as connections between symbols and personal experiences deepen, the reader's confidence and proficiency will grow, solidifying the relationship between shapes and patterns and the intricate stories they narrate.

In modern practice, the integration of technology can enhance these traditional methods of interpretation. Employing tools such as Emacs can facilitate the documentation of readings, allowing practitioners to categorize symbols, develop a personal lexicon, and analyze patterns over time. The ability to draw and depict shapes within software can allow for a more visual approach to interpretation, aiding memorization and understanding.

Finally, continual exploration and openness to interpretation are fundamental. Experimenting with different teas, varying the routine, and engaging with others in the community can foster fresh perspectives and deeper understanding. Since the landscape of tea leaf reading is a living tradition, flexibility in interpretations allows for growth and enrichment, keeping the practice vibrant and in synchrony with the reader's journey.

Through a practice grounded in observation and fluidity, the reader can cultivate a meaningful dialogue with their tea leaves, revealing insights that extend far beyond what is written on the surface—as they decode the unique shapes and patterns, readers uncover not just hidden truths but also pathways to growth, connection, and self-discovery.

5.3. Common Tasseography Symbols

Tea leaf reading, or tasseography, is a mystical practice steeped in tradition and rich with symbolism. As practitioners dive into the intricate world of interpreting tea leaves, they quickly encounter a plethora of symbols that emerge from the patterns formed by the remnants of the tea. Recognizing and understanding these symbols is vital to unlocking the messages hidden within the leaves, guiding readers on their journey of personal insight and connection with the universe.

Among the most frequently referenced symbols are celestial bodies and natural elements. A circle may represent unity and completion, often indicating that a cycle in one's life is closing, while a star is heralded as a beacon of hope, often signaling guidance and direction. Similarly, moon shapes can embody intuition and feminine energy, suggesting a deep connection to one's emotional core. On the other hand, square shapes may symbolize stability and security, calling attention to areas in life that require grounding or balance.

Other symbols reflect more tangible concepts. For instance, a heart indicates love, compassion, and emotional relationships, serving as a powerful reminder of the querent's connections with others. Conversely, a key may signify new opportunities, openings, or discoveries, hinting at forthcoming transitions that lead to greater growth. A tree shape often draws attention to personal development or family ties, encapsulating the depth of ancestry and nurturing relationships.

Shapes depicting water, like waves or a flowing stream, emphasize fluidity and adaptability, indicating a need to embrace change or go with the flow. This could mean the querent ought to let go of rigid plans or expectations, allowing events to unfold naturally. In contrast, mountainous shapes signal strength and resilience, reminding readers to remain steadfast amidst life's challenges.

In the context of social connections and community, symbols like circles or interconnected lines highlight relationships and teamwork, urging readers to assess their social interactions. Such insights can encourage the querent to seek collaboration or reflect on their dynamics with others. These forms outline the importance of communal ties and remind practitioners that interpersonal bonds can profoundly shape one's path.

Animals represented in the tea leaves can add further richness to interpretations. For example, the silhouette of a bird may signal newfound freedom or the arrival of unexpected news, while a snake suggests transformation, shedding old layers to embrace new beginnings. These motifs often elicit instinctual reactions and represent deeper universal archetypes—the recognition of which can heighten the reading experience.

Practitioners should also be mindful of the context in which these symbols appear. Their meanings can evolve based on personal experiences, current life stages, and emotions. Thus, a heart may not only indicate romantic relationships but also symbolize self-love and the nurturing of one's inner child during times of self-reflection.

As tea leaf readers deepen their practices, they may find that their interpretations of common symbols become more nuanced over time, influenced by their experiences, feelings, and interactions with the querent. Keeping a dedicated journal or digital log of readings—utilizing platforms like Emacs—allows practitioners to reflect on and refine their interpretations, tracking how their understanding evolves with their experiences.

Ultimately, tasseography's beauty lies in its subjectivity and the unique connection it fosters between the reader, the symbols, and the querent. By delving into these common symbols and their meanings, practitioners can enhance their interpretations and facilitate deeper insights for themselves and those who seek guidance. The tea leaves may whisper their secrets, but it is through attentive observation and reflection that the true narratives unfold, blending intuition with the art of symbolism to illuminate the path ahead.

5.4. The Effect of Different Brews

Different brews of tea can significantly influence the interpretative experience of tasseography, infusing readings with unique characteristics that are tied to the distinctive properties of each type of tea. The leaves left behind after brewing offer not just a residue, but a nuanced dialogue that can enrich or alter the messages conveyed during readings, rendering it essential to understand how different brews can shape interpretations.

When considering the effects of various tea preparations, it's essential to recognize that the essence of the tea does not merely impact flavor but also the emotional and psychological environment surrounding the reading. Each brew carries its unique historical context, cultural significance, and symbolic associations that can shape the interpretation of the shapes formed by the tea leaves.

Green Tea is often associated with clarity, renewal, and positive transformations. Its lighter brew tends to leave behind fine, delicate leaves that create subtle patterns. Readers engaging with green tea may find that their interpretations lean towards themes of regeneration, growth, and fresh beginnings. The fluidity of patterns formed could suggest adaptability and a call to embrace change. Consequently, readings derived from green tea may encourage querents to reflect on new opportunities emerging in their lives, instilling a sense of hope and vitality.

Black Tea, with its robust flavor and deep color, provides a contrasting experience. The powerful essence of black tea often leads to more pronounced shapes and clearer delineation of symbols. Readers may interpret formations from black tea as significant markers of strength, stability, and determination. A heart shape derived from the rigorously brewed black tea might indicate serious romantic connections or firm commitments, suggesting that emotions run deep and require attention. The bold character of the tea contributes to a feeling of groundedness in readings, often prompting extensions into themes of challenge, perseverance, and the need to confront life's difficulties head-on.

Oolong Tea, known for its semi-oxidation, occupies a fascinating middle ground between the traits associated with green and black tea. When brewed properly, oolong reveals a diverse range of flavors and aromas. The leaves' shapes may represent duality and balance, hinting at the viewer's ability to navigate between contrasting situations. Their formations might suggest that querents embrace their challenges while remaining open to new experiences. The tea may indicate a time of transition, encouraging readers to reflect on how they can harmonize diverging paths in their lives.

Herbal Teas add yet another layer of complexity in tasseography. Depending on the specific herbs used, these brews could imbue readings with a multitude of meanings—often tied to the properties associated with the individual herbs. For instance, chamomile is synonymous with relaxation, inviting peaceful reflections; while peppermint may symbolize clarity and swift change. Due to their varying compositions, herbal teas can produce diverse patterns, offering a wide range of interpretations that reflect the querent's emotional states or health concerns. When herbal leaves are examined, the reader may discern meanings tied to self-care, wellness, and renewal, inviting the querent to engage in introspection on these themes.

White Tea, known for its gentle nature and health benefits, brings a sense of purity and simplicity into readings. Readers engaging with white tea often find that the patterns left behind are delicate and refined, embodying themes of innocence and spiritual enlightenment. Interpretations may lend toward encouraging a return to one's core values or highlighting the importance of authenticity in interactions with others. The clarity of shapes drawn from white tea may suggest that the reader or querent is emerging towards a deeper understanding of self.

The method of preparation also plays a crucial role. The temperature and steeping time can alter the extraction of flavors and compounds from the leaves, influencing their shapes and the emotional tone set for the reading. For example, a rushed brew with boiling water may yield bitter leaves with chaotic forms, potentially heralding confusion or conflict, while a slow infusion with lower temperatures creates a more harmonious experience, gently allowing the patterns to emerge.

Furthermore, the environmental context of the reading can shape its interpretations as well. A serene atmosphere complemented by a gentle brew can foster mindfulness, encouraging richer engagement with symbolism. Conversely, an energetic space accompanied by robust tea may lead to more intense interpretations, as emotional vibrations from both tea and surroundings intertwine during the reading process.

In conclusion, the interplay between different brews and their subsequent effects on tea leaf readings highlights the nuance of tasseography as a practice that embodies both art and science. Practitioners should carefully consider the type of tea they choose, as well as how it is prepared, to further facilitate deep connections with the symbols and messages unveiled in their readings. Understanding the influence of various brews cultivates a more profound sense of mindfulness and enriches the journey of tea leaf reading, offering practitioners a broader spectrum of interpretation and insight from the tea leaves that tell their stories.

5.5. From Preparation to Interpretation

In the practice of tasseography, understanding the journey from the preparation of tea to the interpretation of the leaves is essential for unlocking the depths of meaning contained within each reading. This multifaceted process begins with the selection and brewing of tea, which establishes the foundation for the reading experience, allowing the reader to connect with both the physical and metaphysical dimensions of this ancient art.

The first step in the journey is choosing the right type of tea. Each variety—whether black, green, herbal, oolong, or white—carries its own unique properties and significance that can enhance the reading. When selecting your tea, consider not only personal preference but also the symbolic meanings associated with each brew. Black tea, for example, is robust and assertive, often suggesting themes of strength and perseverance, while green tea is light and fresh, evoking feelings of clarity and new beginnings. The tea ritual becomes a conduit for the reader's intentions, aligning their mindset with the qualities inherent to the chosen tea.

Preparing the tea involves mindful attention. The temperature of the water, the steeping time, and the amount of leaves used all contribute to the potency of the infusion. A well-brewed cup captures the essence of the leaves, creating a richer experience during interpretation. As you brew your tea, take a moment to focus on your intentions for the reading. This meditative approach establishes a connection between the external world and your internal state, fostering an atmosphere conducive to divination.

Once the tea has steeped appropriately, pour the liquid into a cup, leaving at least a spoonful of the wet leaves at the bottom. Some practitioners prefer to turn the cup upside down on a saucer after enjoying the tea, allowing the leaves to settle into patterns. This moment marks the transition from preparation to interpretation, where the leaves transform from a mere residue to a canvas of symbols.

As you begin to interpret the shapes formed by the leaves, observe their arrangement and context within the cup. Look for distinctive patterns, such as circles, lines, and angles, and consider their meanings. A circle, for example, may symbolize wholeness or completion, while a straight line can suggest direction and clarity. Pay attention to the density and spread of the leaves, as this can also influence your interpretations. A concentrated mass of leaves might represent urgency or intensity in a specific area of life, while scattered leaves could indicate flexibility or an element of unpredictability.

While interpreting the shapes, trust your intuition. The beauty of tasseography lies in its ability to connect the reader to their own insights. Different symbols may evoke distinct feelings or memories, so embrace your personal associations with each shape. It's essential to recognize the subjective nature of interpretation; while there are common meanings attributed to various shapes, each reader's context and experiences will shape their understanding uniquely.

Record your interpretations in real-time, taking notes in a journal or, for example, using Emacs to document insights digitally. This practice not only reinforces your interpretations but also allows you to revisit and reflect on them later. Over time, you can track patterns and recurring symbols that appear in your readings, deepening your understanding and connection to the symbols the leaves reveal.

Finally, the journey does not end with interpretation; it extends into action. The insights gained from reading the tea leaves can inform personal decisions, goals, and relationships. Reflect on how the symbols resonate within the broader context of your life, and consider how you might apply the guidance indicated by the leaves. Engaging in this reflective process turns tea leaf reading from a passive experience into a dynamic relationship with your intuition and the world around you.

In conclusion, the journey from preparation to interpretation encompasses a spectrum of intentional practices, mindful observations, and intuitive interpretations. By embracing the entire process—from selecting the right tea to reflecting on the insights gained—you transform the ritual of tea leaf reading into a powerful tool for self-discovery and personal growth. As practitioners navigate each step with care and mindfulness, they unlock the potential hidden within each cup, allowing the leaves to impart their wisdom and illuminate paths forward in life.

6. Tools to Enhance Your Reading Experience

6.1. Selecting the Right Tools and Utensils

Selecting the right tools and utensils for tea leaf reading is crucial to enhancing the practice experience and ensuring insightful interpretations. A well-chosen selection of items will not only aid the reading process but also create an inviting atmosphere conducive to reflection and creativity. This section provides an in-depth guide to choosing the best types of cups and accessories for those engaging in this mystic art.

At the heart of tea leaf reading is the cup itself. The type of cup used plays a significant role in how the leaves perform and ultimately how the interpretations manifest. Traditionally, many practitioners prefer using a delicate teacup that allows the leaves to settle artistically, forming clear patterns that can be easily observed. Porcelain cups are often favored for their smooth surfaces and aesthetic appeal, as they not only enhance the visual beauty of the tea but also help maintain the ideal temperature for steeping the tea. When selecting a cup, look for one with a wide brim that encourages the leaves to stretch out and create distinctive shapes.

Furthermore, consider choosing a cup with a transparent or semi-transparent body. This feature allows for a visual appreciation of the leaves during and after the brewing process, which can enhance the reader's connection to the symbols formed. Clear glass cups can provide spectacular views of the swirling leaves, making the reading experience more engaging and immersive. Alternatively, some practitioners may prefer decorative cups adorned with intricate designs or motifs that resonate personally, adding a layer of symbolism and intention to the readings.

The material with which the cup is crafted also carries significant implications for the reading. Each material can influence the flavor profile and temperature retention of the tea, thereby affecting the experience of the leaves. In addition to porcelain and glass, clay cups can yield a unique charm during readings. Unglazed clay vessels, often used in traditional tea ceremonies, can contribute to a more earthy, grounded feel, allowing the practice to connect with natural elements. This choice often resonates with those who prefer a holistic approach to their spiritual practices.

Equally important is the choice of tea itself. The type of tea leaves used contributes uniquely to the shapes formed and the meanings derived from them. Select a tea that parallels the themes you wish to explore in your reading. For instance, if seeking clarity or insight, green tea may serve well; its light flavors and fresh nuances foster a sense of renewal. In contrast, rich black teas can ground the reader, typically associated with strength and stability, and may provide profound insights into emotional depths.

To further enrich the reading experience, consider incorporating additional utensils such as a tea infuser or strainer, particularly when using loose leaf teas. These tools allow you to enjoy the full flavor of the tea while also promoting easy cleanup and maintaining the clarity of the readings. Selecting a simple yet effective infuser ensures that the leaves steep evenly without creating muddled flavors, resulting in a smooth cup that captures the essence of the tea and allows for the optimal presentation of the leaves.

To cultivate the right ambiance for tea leaf reading, creating a serene environment is essential. Equip your space with soft lighting, candles, or incense to enhance the sensory experience. Combining the physical tools with this ambient setting promotes a relaxed state, facilitating a deeper connection with the practice. A tranquil environment encourages mindfulness and intentionality—elements that are crucial for successful tea leaf reading.

Additionally, consider a dedicated notebook or journal to document the readings and reflect upon the insights gained. Recording your interpretations not only serves as a reference for future readings but also helps track personal reflections and growth over time. Using software like Emacs to manage and organize your notes can streamline this process, enabling easy access to past insights and reinforcing the connection between the symbols and your personal journey.

As you prepare your space, balance the presence of traditional elements with modern conveniences. A clean, organized approach ensures that your tools are easy to access, while also creating a visually appealing workspace that invites you into the ritual of tea leaf reading.

In summary, selecting the right tools and utensils is a foundational step in developing a meaningful tea leaf reading practice. By thoughtfully choosing your cup, tea, and accessories, you set the stage for insightful interpretations and personal growth. This process encourages a harmonious integration of tradition and contemporary practices, enhancing both the mystical and transformative aspects of tasseography. Embrace the opportunity to curate your tools mindfully, as they will serve as essential partners on your journey into the world of tea leaf reading.

6.2. Using Technology to Record Readings

Using technology can significantly enhance the practice of recording tea leaf readings, bridging the gap between traditional mysticism and modern analytical methods. By integrating tools that streamline and structure the reading process, practitioners can document their experiences effectively while ensuring that insights gathered from the tea leaves are preserved for future reflection. This marriage of ancient art and contemporary technology opens up new avenues for understanding and personal growth in the realm of tasseography.

One of the most powerful digital tools available to practitioners is Emacs, a highly customizable text editor beloved by programmers. Its versatility allows readers not just to create simple documentation logs but to develop a complex interactive environment tailored specifically for their tea leaf readings. By leveraging Emacs' powerful capabilities, practitioners can dictate the parameters of their journeys, shaping personalized experiences that cultivate deeper connections with the meanings behind their readings.

To begin with, using Emacs to record readings opens up multiple methods of documentation. Practitioners can create organized log entries, complete with details about the type of tea used, the date of the reading, and descriptions of the symbols formed by the leaves. These entries can be structured using Org mode, which facilitates hierarchical organization and tagging, enabling readers to categorize their notes based on themes or recurring symbols. This transformation of handwritten notes into a structured digital format not only aids in accessibility but also offers an easy way to revisit past readings, fostering a deeper understanding over time.

Additionally, technology enables enhanced note-taking practices. Readers can document real-time reflections as they engage with the symbols, capturing spontaneous insights that may otherwise be lost. This active engagement encourages mindfulness during the reading process, allowing for holistic contemplation of the shapes formed. By recording personalized interpretations, practitioners can begin to trace their own emotional landscapes and thought processes—an invaluable tool for personal growth and self-awareness.

Moreover, the ability to integrate visual elements into digital records elevates the practice to new heights. Users can incorporate photographs of the tea leaves, sketches, or even digital representations of the symbols into their notes, creating a visually stimulating experience that deepens the connection with the readings. Having a visual reference can provide clarity, allowing readers to engage with their interpretations in a way that abstract words cannot convey alone. Such dynamic records cement the relationship between symbols and their meanings, reinforcing readers' intuitive understanding as they contemplate the narratives the leaves reveal.

Digital tools also pave the way for a community-centered approach to tea leaf reading. Embracing technology means practitioners can share their readings and insights with fellow enthusiasts through various online platforms. By harnessing social media and forums dedicated to tasseography and divination, practitioners can connect with others, exchange interpretations, and even discuss varying symbolic meanings. This collaborative spirit not only enriches individuals' practices but strengthens the collective understanding of the art of tasseography, allowing for the sharing of diverse perspectives and experiences.

For those who might find themselves doubting their interpretations or questioning their intuitive practices, digital documentation offers an opportunity for reflection and analysis. By revisiting past readings and examining their handwritten or typed notes, users can track their personal growth, observe recurring themes, and affirm the accuracy of their interpretations against real life events. This alignment of insights with lived experiences can bolster confidence in one's abilities and deepen the overall understanding of the tea leaf reading process.

Yet, while the advent of technology introduces numerous benefits, it's essential to maintain a balance between digital tools and the intimate, personal nature of tea leaf reading. While recording and analyzing readings, practitioners must remember the essence of tassography— the art of intuition and reflection. This principle encourages readers to remain connected to the organic experience of reading tea leaves, ensuring that technology complements rather than supplants the intrinsic qualities of the practice.

In conclusion, the integration of technology into the recording and analysis of tea leaf readings heralds a new age for practitioners—one that honors tradition while embracing modernity. By utilizing tools like Emacs to document and reflect on their readings, individuals can cultivate deeper insights and narratives from their tea leaves while engaging with a larger community of fellow practitioners. This synergy not only enhances the richness of the reading experience but ultimately leads to transformative journeys of self-discovery and connection, illuminating the path forward through the wisdom of the leaves and the clarity of digital documentation.

6.3. Supplementing Tasseography with Digital Tools

Supplementing Tasseography with Digital Tools opens up a world of possibilities for practitioners, merging the ancient art of tea leaf reading with the advantages of modern technology. As individuals embrace innovative approaches to traditional practices, the integration of digital tools not only enriches the experience but also encourages a deeper exploration of the insights hidden in tea leaves.

From recording readings to accessing a broader array of symbols, the utilization of technology allows for a more structured, reflective, and insightful process. Digital platforms, particularly software like Emacs, empower readers by providing diverse functionalities to assist in the meticulous act of documentation and analysis. Emacs can serve as a personalized hub where one can log readings, categorize insights, and visualize recurring patterns over time.

To begin with, using Emacs facilitates the organization of notes related to tea leaf readings. Practitioners can create structured templates that encapsulate crucial information about each reading, such as the date, type of tea used, and individual interpretations of the symbols gleaned from the leaves. This system of recording provides a coherent narrative surrounding each reading, enabling practitioners to refer back to their discoveries and reflect on their evolving insights.

Moreover, the ability to categorize and tag entries creates a rich database of experiences that allow for more profound analysis. Utilizing features like Org mode within Emacs, readers can develop a personal lexicon of symbols, complete with meanings and associations. As they document their readings, practitioners can easily reference previous interpretations and assess how their understanding has shifted over time, reinforcing the connection between personal experiences and the insights derived from tea leaves.

Visual aids play a critical role in enhancing the tea leaf reading process. Employing digital tools enables the inclusion of photographs or sketches alongside textual notes, inviting a more nuanced way to engage with the interpretations. By capturing the distinct shapes formed by the leaves and documenting personal reflections, readers create a visual repository that complements their written insights.

This blend of visual and textual elements invites a holistic approach to understanding the unique narratives each reading offers.

Community engagement also flourishes within the digital sphere. Online platforms and social media allow practitioners of tasseography to share their experiences, techniques, and interpretations of tea leaves with one another. This interconnectedness not only fosters a sense of belonging but also enhances individual learning as readers exchange varying perspectives on symbols and readings. Communities that form around these digital tools provide invaluable support, enabling practitioners to explore different interpretations and deepen their understanding of the reading process.

However, while technology enhances the reading experience, it is vital for practitioners to maintain the integrity of the ritual. The essence of tasseography relies on the intuitive and emotional connections forged during readings. Balancing the use of digital tools while honoring the traditional aspects of tea leaf reading ensures that the practice remains grounded in its historical and cultural roots.

In conclusion, supplementing tasseography with digital tools encourages practitioners to explore new horizons in tea leaf reading. By embracing technology, individuals can streamline their documentation processes, engage more fully with personal insights, and connect with a broader community of fellow readers. The integration of these elements does not diminish the art of tasseography; instead, it revitalizes the practice, inviting both seasoned readers and newcomers to discover the wisdom contained within the teacups. As practitioners navigate this evolving landscape, they merge the beauty of tradition with the promise of innovation, drawing from the profound truths found in tea leaves while forging paths of understanding with modern conveniences.

6.4. Creating a Personal Space for Tea Sessions

Creating a personal space for tea sessions is an essential step in cultivating an environment conducive to the introspective practice of tea leaf reading, or tasseography. This process involves not just the physical setup but also the emotional and mental atmosphere that the space could foster—one that invites reflection, connection, and interpretation as leaves settle into forms that carry potential insights. A well-designed personal space allows practitioners to immerse themselves in the ritual, deepening their engagement with the readings and ensuring a holistic approach to this ancient art.

To begin with, the location of your tea-reading space should be a place that feels safe and inviting. Whether it's a cozy corner of a room, a dedicated reading nook, or even a small garden setup, the importance of creating a space that resonates with comfort cannot be overstated. Choose an area that you can accessorize with items that personalize the environment, such as meaningful artwork, plants, or textiles that evoke warmth and calmness. Surrounding yourself with familiar elements helps ground the practice, allowing for mindfulness to flourish.

Next, consider the significance of lighting. The ambiance of your tea-reading space can be greatly enhanced by the light you choose to utilize. Soft, natural lighting that mimics daylight can create an uplifting and serene atmosphere that complements the reflective nature of tasseography. If natural light is limited in your chosen location, consider using warm-toned lamps or candles that provide gentle illumination, fostering a tranquil environment that encourages contemplation and relaxation. Dimming the lights slightly can enhance the overall experience, allowing you to focus on the symbols that emerge from the tea leaves without external distractions.

Sound also plays a significant role in shaping your personal tea-reading space. The auditory environment should be soothing and conducive to focus. Incorporating gentle background music—perhaps instrumental?—or sounds of nature, like flowing water or birdsong, can enhance the meditation aspect of tea leaf readings. Soundscapes serve to neutralize outside distractions and invite deeper immersion into the tea ritual. For those who prefer silence, consider incorporating a white noise machine or a subtle fan to drown out any disruptive sounds that may disrupt your focus.

Another critical aspect of your personal space is ensuring that all the necessary utensils and materials are readily accessible. A well-organized area should include your chosen teacups, tea selections, infusers, and an inviting teapot. Having these tools at hand can streamline your preparation process, allowing you to dive directly into the ritual of tea leaf reading. Maintaining a notebook or digital tool like Emacs close by can facilitate the documentation of impressions and insights as they arise, ensuring that reflections can be captured without interrupting the flow of the reading.

Additionally, consider integrating elements that ignite the senses. Fresh flowers, herbs, or incense can introduce delightful fragrances that elevate the tea-drinking experience. These sensory enhancements can not only create a pleasant ambiance but also invite feelings that align with the intentions behind the reading. For example, burning sage might evoke cleansing energies, while chamomile essential oil may promote relaxation and quietude.

Personalizing your space with tokens of inspiration or symbolism can also deepen your connection to the practice. This could be as simple as displaying crystals, meaningful artifacts, or photographs that resonate with you, invoking intentions or facilitating a sense of presence. As you read the leaves, these items serve as reminders of your aspirations, guiding you back to your intentions as you interpret the tea leaves before you.

It may be beneficial to incorporate a ritualistic approach to your tea sessions. Establishing a routine that precedes your readings can condition your mind and body to enter a space of mindfulness. This could involve simple practices such as meditation, breathing exercises, or gratitude reflections before you begin your readings. Engaging in these preparatory rituals creates a mental shift that elevates your experience, nurturing both focus and receptiveness as you engage with the tea leaves.

Finally, maintaining a clean and organized space cannot be overlooked. A clutter-free environment provides clarity and reduces distractions, allowing you to concentrate fully on your readings. Periodically assess your reading space, decluttering items that no longer resonate or organizing tools that may have shifted. This conscious curation not only refreshes the space but fosters a sense of ownership and connection between the practitioner and their tea rituals.

In conclusion, creating a personal space for tea sessions encapsulates more than just physical arrangement; it embodies the synthesis of intention, emotion, and practicality. By designing a tranquil, sensory-rich environment that prioritizes comfort and focus, practitioners can cultivate an intimate space that enhances their connection to the art of tasseography. This sacred space becomes a conduit for journeying inward through the reflections found in tea leaves, promoting self-discovery and enriching the ancient practice of tea leaf reading with every session. It is within this thoughtfully crafted environment that you can truly immerse yourself in the wisdom and mystery brewed within each cup.

6.5. Balancing Technology and Tradition

The practice of balancing technology and tradition in the realm of tasseography represents a captivating intersection between the ancient art of tea leaf reading and modern methods of documentation and analysis. As practitioners navigate this unique blend, the desire to maintain the essence of the practice while leveraging contemporary tools becomes integral to enhancing the depth and breadth of their readings.

Tasseography, with its rich historical roots, has served as a means for individuals to gain insights into their lives through the interpretation of shapes formed by tea leaves in a cup. Traditionally, this practice was deeply personal, often occurring in intimate settings, where thoughts were shared over a warm cup of tea. The serene atmosphere allowed readers to tap into their intuition and reflect on the symbolism revealed before them. As such, transitioning this practice into the modern world brings forth the challenge of preserving the spirit of tasseography while embracing the benefits of technology.

Modern technology introduces numerous advantages to enhance the ritual of tea leaf reading. Digital tools like Emacs, known for its flexibility and customization, can transform the way practitioners document their experiences. By creating an organized system where insights can be recorded, categorized, and reflected upon, readers can engage with their tea leaf interpretations on a deeper level. For instance, users might develop personalized templates that streamline the logging of readings, making it easier to track patterns and recurring symbols over time. This process fosters a sense of structure that complements the intuitive aspects of the practice, creating harmony between the analytical and the mystical.

Moreover, employing technology facilitates broader community engagement. Online platforms allow practitioners to share their experiences and interpretations with a global audience, fostering a sense of belonging and collective learning. In this digital landscape, individuals can exchange insights, discuss varying symbol meanings, and learn from one another, ultimately enriching their understanding of tasseography. By connecting with a wider community, readers deepen their connection to the practice and discover innovative approaches that enhance their ritual.

However, while integrating technology into this age-old practice presents exciting possibilities, it is crucial for practitioners to remain grounded in the foundational principles of tasseography. The act of reading tea leaves requires mindfulness, intuition, and a personal connection to the symbols presented. Balancing the use of technology without overshadowing the inherent spirit of tea leaf reading is essential. Practitioners should approach technology as a supportive tool rather than a replacement for the rich emotional and spiritual experience that tea leaf reading offers.

Another important facet of balancing tradition and technology is recognizing the potential for reinterpretation. As readers encounter new symbols or evolve their understanding of established ones, the adaptability of the practice becomes apparent. Embracing modern insights while respecting traditional interpretations can lead to fresh perspectives on the meanings behind tea leaves. This iterative process allows the practice to remain dynamic, in tune with the changing lives of its practitioners, while honoring its historical roots.

Practicing mindfulness during readings becomes paramount in this balance. Setting intentions, cultivating a sacred space, and engaging in meditative practices prior to each reading keeps the focus on the symbolism of the tea leaves rather than becoming overwhelmed by the tools at hand. Maintaining a reflective and open mindset strengthens the connection to both the practice and the tools used within it. By ensuring that technology serves as an enhancement rather than a distraction, practitioners can enjoy a deeper understanding of their experiences.

In essence, balancing technology and tradition within the context of tasseography allows practitioners to enjoy the best of both worlds. It emphasizes the importance of preserving the essence of tea leaf reading while embracing the innovative possibilities offered by modern tools. By nurturing personal insight, fostering community engagement, and practicing mindfulness, individuals can enjoy a richer, more fulfilling journey into the world of tasseography. This balance represents a beautiful synthesis between past and present—a merging of historical wisdom with contemporary expression, inviting practitioners to explore new horizons in this ancient art.

7. Mindful Approaches to Tea Leaf Reading

7.1. The Spirit of Mindfulness in Divination

In the realm of tea leaf reading, the spirit of mindfulness becomes an essential companion, enriching the experience and deepening one's connection to the art of tasseography. Mindfulness, rooted in the practice of being present and fully engaged with one's thoughts, emotions, and surroundings, enhances the ritual of reading tea leaves by fostering a conscious and intentional approach to both interpretation and self-reflection. This harmony between awareness and intuition transforms tea leaf reading from a mere divination exercise into a profound journey of self-discovery and insight.

At the heart of the mindfulness approach is the cultivation of a present moment awareness that encourages practitioners to step away from the distractions of daily life. Prior to engaging in a reading, it is important to create a designated space that promotes serenity and reduces external disturbances. This environmental preparation sets the tone for focusing on the task at hand. It could involve dimming the lights, lighting candles, or playing gentle background music—elements that contribute to creating an atmosphere of tranquility conducive to mindfulness.

Mindfully approaching tea leaf reading invites users to attune their senses, paying attention to the aroma of the tea and the intricate dance of the leaves in the cup. As tea is consumed and the leaves settle, practitioners are invited to observe not only the shapes that emerge but also their emotional responses to those forms. This heightened awareness allows for an exploration of intuition, where interpretations are informed by not just the visual patterns but also by the immediate feelings evoked in the moment.

Incorporating breathing exercises before starting the reading can further enhance mindfulness. Deep, deliberate breaths promote calmness and enhance focus, creating a bridge between mental clarity and intuitive insights. By anchoring attention to the breath, individuals can release tension and open up to the possibilities that lie within the teacup. This preparatory ritual encourages individuals to be fully present, embracing the art of interpretation with an open heart and mind.

Throughout the reading process, mindfulness becomes vital in maintaining a balance between objectivity and intuition. While tea leaf readings often come with established meanings attached to certain symbols, being open to personal interpretations allows practitioners to dive deeper into their subconscious minds. The symbols may resonate with unique personal experiences or current life circumstances, revealing insights that go beyond traditional interpretations. Mindfulness assists in discerning the layers of meaning hidden within the leaves, encouraging practitioners to trust their intuitive responses while remaining aware of the concrete symbolism presented by the tea leaves.

Equipped with tools like Emacs, practitioners can facilitate mindfulness in their practices through organized documentation and reflection. Emacs allows for an elegant way to log readings, track patterns over time, and preserve the journey of self-discovery revealed in the tea. By maintaining structured notes, individuals can foster an ongoing dialogue with their experiences, where mindfulness is not confined to the moment of reading but extends into ongoing reflection.

Lastly, the practice of mindfulness transforms tea leaf reading into a transformative ritual that encourages personal growth. As practitioners dive deeply into their readings, they may uncover not only insights related to their futures but also self-awareness and understanding of their emotions, desires, and challenges. This process fosters resilience and adaptability as they learn to navigate life's ebbs and flows through the guidance of tea leaves.

In essence, embracing the spirit of mindfulness within tea leaf reading enriches the practice, forging a connection between the reader, the leaves, and the wisdom hidden within. By nurturing awareness and sensitivity during readings, practitioners can unlock profound insights, embracing the journey of self-discovery as they unveil the potential encoded in every sip of tea.

7.2. Preparing Mentally and Spiritually

To prepare for a successful tea leaf reading, it is essential to engage in both mental and spiritual practices that align with the reflective nature of this ancient art. Mindfulness is at the heart of this preparation, centering your thoughts and emotions to create an inviting space for intuitive insights to arise. In the journey through tasseography, the ability to harness your mental clarity and spiritual intent directly facilitates a deeper connection with the messages hidden within the tea leaves.

The first step in preparing mentally involves a focused intention-setting ritual. Before your reading, take a moment to silence your mind, setting aside distractions and external worries. This can be achieved through a brief meditation session, during which you can close your eyes, take several deep breaths, and visualize yourself entering a peaceful state of awareness. Picture the tea leaves in your cup revealing their symbols and stories, and invite the energies of intuition and wisdom into your readings. As you breathe in, focus on inviting clarity; as you breathe out, let go of any tension or preconceived notions you may hold about the interpretations.

Practicing gratitude can further enhance your mental state. Reflect on the significance of the tea leaves, the ritual of brewing, and the opportunity to connect with your inner self through this practice. Expressing gratitude serves to elevate your vibration and openness to receiving insights, ensuring that you approach the reading with a receptive heart and mind.

In conjunction with mental preparation, nurturing a spiritual connection sets the stage for a more profound reading experience. Engaging with rituals that honor your spiritual beliefs can foster a sense of unity with the universe. This could involve lighting candles, burning sage, or placing crystals in your space—tools that carry energies conducive to divination. As you perform these rituals, visualize the cumulative intentions you release into the universe, calling upon guidance from higher realms to support your readings.

For many practitioners, creating a sacred space enhances the spiritual aspect of the practice. Designate an area specifically for tea leaf reading, filled with items that hold significance for you—such as inspirational quotes, symbols, or meaningful artifacts. This sacred temple can serve not just as a physical space but also as an emotional sanctuary where you can retreat for introspection.

In addition to creating an inviting atmosphere, incorporating meditative practices into your routine can further strengthen your mental and spiritual alignment prior to a reading. These practices may range from deep breathing exercises to guided visualizations. Even something as simple as sitting in silence for a few moments to connect with your breath can shift your focus from external noise to inward clarity. Emphasis on stillness invites a deeper awareness of the present moment, where interpretations can resonate authentically, allowing the tea leaves to communicate their insights freely.

Balancing objectivity with intuition is a key aspect of effective tea leaf reading. While analyzing the shapes, it's essential to remain grounded in rational thought while also engaging with your intuitive self. Training yourself to discern between analytical observation and intuitive flashes can elevate the quality of your interpretations.

With Emacs as a tool, you can enhance your focus during readings. Design your Emacs environment to exclude distraction, keeping notes from past readings at your fingertips, and providing space to jot down new insights as they arise. This combination of mental engagement, spiritual connection, and practical organization strengthens your reading practice, elevating it from mere observation to a sacred ritual that informs and transforms.

In summary, preparing mentally and spiritually for tea leaf readings involves a thoughtful interplay of intention-setting, mindfulness, ritual, and environment. By embracing these practices, you cultivate a receptive mindset that allows for profound insights to emerge during your encounters with the tea leaves. Ultimately, this holistic preparation transforms the art of tasseography into a meaningful journey of self-discovery—a compelling narrative that intertwines your inner world with the mystique of the tea leaves before you.

7.3. Meditative Practices Before a Reading

Meditative practices before a reading create an essential foundation for connecting with the tea leaves and harnessing the innate insights they may convey. By integrating intention and mindfulness, these practices orient the mind and spirit towards a receptive and profound experience during the tea leaf reading ritual. As you prepare for this intimate encounter with the leaves, consider the following detailed meditative techniques that can enhance your experience.

Begin your meditation by selecting a quiet space where you feel comfortable and free from distractions. This space can be adorned with elements that inspire calmness—such as candles, crystals, or plants—that resonate with you. Grounding your environment helps to establish a sacred atmosphere conducive to the practices ahead. Settle into your chosen seat, either on a cushion or a chair, ensuring that your posture reflects both comfort and alertness.

Start by closing your eyes and taking several deep breaths. Inhale through your nose, allowing your diaphragm to expand fully, and then exhale gently through your mouth. This rhythm of breath is vital as it signals the body to relax and prepares the mind to focus on the moment. Repeat this breathing pattern, visualizing the inhalation as a wave of calm sweeping over you, washing away distractions and stresses accumulated throughout your day.

After a few moments of focused breathing, fold in a practice of intention-setting. With your eyes still closed, reflect on the purpose of your upcoming reading. What questions or themes do you wish to explore? These intentions can be broad, such as seeking clarity, guidance, or understanding, or they can be more specific, touching on particular life events or concerns. Once you have crafted a clear intention, visualize it forming a gentle light or energy that radiates from your heart center, expanding outward into your space. This light symbolizes your openness to the insights the tea leaves may reveal.

This moment of intention-setting moves seamlessly into a brief mindfulness meditation. Begin to engage with the sensory experience surrounding you. Pay attention to the sounds in the background — the gentle rustle of leaves, the distant hum of everyday life, or even the soft chime of a clock. Embrace them without judgment, letting them become part of your meditation. Next, draw your focus to the scent of the tea you will be using. Inhale deeply, allowing the aroma to fill your senses and transport you into a tranquil state. This sensory engagement helps anchor you in the present moment and aligns your mind with the ritual to come.

Once you feel grounded in your meditation, it can be beneficial to take a moment to visualize the tea leaves in your cup. Envision them swirling gently in the water, releasing their essence and transforming into shapes and patterns. Picture yourself inviting wisdom from these leaves, understanding that they contain not only the history of the tea but also the energy of your intentions. This visualization reinforces the connection between you and the elements you will soon interpret.

As you transition from meditation into the actual reading, consider maintaining a light-hearted focus, akin to a gentle curiosity about what the tea leaves may reveal. This mindset allows for fluidity in interpretation, welcoming whatever shapes and insights emerge without judgment or expectations. If any anxieties or doubts surface concerning the readings, acknowledge them, and gently redirect your focus back to your intention and the visualization of the tea leaves.

After this preparatory meditation, allow yourself a moment to adjust your physical space as you prepare the tea. Begin the ritual of brewing with the intention you have refined during your meditation. While the tea steeps, remain aware of your breath and any lingering sensations from your meditative practice, allowing them to enhance your connection to the experience. As the leaves settle in the cup, carry with you the sense of calm and clarity cultivated during your meditative session.

By consistently incorporating these meditative practices before tea leaf readings, you enhance not only the experience itself but also your ability to connect with your inner wisdom. The tea leaves transform from simple remnants of a beverage into meaningful symbols, guided by your mindfulness and intention. This synergy of mind, body, and spirit unfurls the potential for insights that are both profound and illuminating, making each reading a cherished journey into self-discovery.

7.4. Balancing Objectivity and Intuition

In the practice of tea leaf reading, achieving a balance between objectivity and intuition is a nuanced journey that elevates the reading experience. While the art of tasseography possesses a rich tapestry of symbolism that can inform interpretations, the personal insights and intuitive flashes of the reader play an equally vital role. This delicate interplay allows practitioners to draw meaning from both the objective shapes left by the tea leaves and the subjectivity of their interpretations, resulting in a more comprehensive understanding of the insights the tea offers.

To begin with, it's important to recognize the distinct qualities of objectivity and intuition. Objectivity in tea leaf reading relies on established symbolism, where specific shapes and forms carry traditional meanings. For instance, a heart may signify love or emotional connections, a key often points towards new opportunities, and a star symbolizes hope or guidance. Understanding these symbols allows the practitioner to ground their readings in a common lexicon that can be communicated effectively.

However, reliance solely on traditional interpretations could potentially limit the reading's depth. This is where intuition steps into the reading process. Each individual reader brings their own unique context, experiences, and emotional resonances to the act of interpretation. Intuition allows practitioners to tap into their personal insights and nuanced feelings associated with the shapes formed by the tea leaves. This process necessitates letting go of rigid frameworks, allowing the reader to explore the richness of personal connections to the symbols.

One effective method to cultivate this balancing act is by approaching the reading with mindfulness. Practitioners can establish a clear intention prior to drinking the tea, setting the stage for a reflective process. As the tea is consumed, taking mental note of the sensations, emotions, and thoughts that arise creates a dynamic interplay between objective observation and personal reflection. This mindful engagement cultivates receptivity, allowing intuitive insights to surface naturally as the leaves settle in the cup.

It's also valuable for readers to document their findings in a way that unites both objective observations and intuitive impressions. Utilizing a tool like Emacs for note-taking not only provides a structured approach to logging readings but allows space for non-linear thoughts and associations as well. Readers can create sections in their documents for traditional symbols alongside reflections, tapping into their inherent connections to the interpretations. This amalgamation deepens the reading, blending the analytical with the intuitive.

Additionally, engaging with the symbols in a symbiotic manner can bolster one's ability to balance objectivity and intuition. After identifying established meanings from the symbols formed by the leaves, practitioners can ask themselves how those symbols resonate with their own experiences. For instance, if a crescent moon appears in the reading, they might reflect on what it signifies in terms of their personal life and emotions. This incorporation of personal narratives not only leads to deeper insights but also enhances the relevance of the reading to their lived experiences.

While embracing subjectivity is crucial, readers should remember the value of grounding their interpretations in objectivity. This doesn't mean dismissing intuition; rather, it's about creating a harmonious relationship between both. Acknowledging that the shapes of the leaves may potentially bear significance tied to broader life contexts while allowing the emotional responses to guide the interpretations fosters a holistic approach to reading.

Lastly, engaging with a community of tea leaf readers can provide further insights in achieving this balance. Sharing experiences, interpretations, and perspectives within a supportive network can enrich readers' comprehension of the symbols and their meanings. The collective wisdom gleaned from discussions fosters collaborative growth that ultimately enhances each reader's ability to navigate the intricate relationship between objectivity and intuition.

Ultimately, balancing objectivity and intuition in tea leaf reading amplifies the quality of the practice. This equilibrium invites readers to explore depths of meaning that extend beyond the surface of the leaves into a realm infused with personal resonance and emotional truth. By embracing both perspectives, practitioners enhance their readings, uncovering profound insights that guide them on their journeys of self-discovery. This delicate interplay not only honors the practice of tasseography but also invites practitioners to enhance their interpretations, illuminating life's mysteries revealed through the humble medium of tea leaves.

7.5. Enhancing Focus with Emacs

Enhancing focus during tea leaf reading can be greatly supported by the unique capabilities of Emacs, a powerful tool known for its customizability and vast array of features that promote an organized and distraction-free environment. In a world full of distractions, creating a focused reading practice becomes essential to gain insights from the tea leaves, and Emacs provides the perfect platform for this endeavor.

To start, one of the key aspects of using Emacs to enhance focus is the ability to create a personalized workspace tailored to your tea reading rituals. This can be achieved by setting up specific buffers, organizing them to separate different elements of your readings—such as one for logging notes, another for tracking recurring symbols, and yet another for reflections. By creating a structured workspace, you minimize the clutter often found in traditional text editors, allowing your mind to concentrate on the task at hand: interpreting the tea leaves.

Utilizing Emacs' powerful Org mode is an effective way to streamline note-taking during readings. With this tool, you can easily format your notes, create lists, and draw important connections between interpretations and the tea leaves you encounter. The hierarchical structure offered by Org mode allows you to categorize insights efficiently, making it simple to refer back to previous readings when you need to recognize patterns or themes in your practice. Managing your notes in an organized way not only enhances clarity but also reinforces focus as you develop a deeper relationship with the symbolic meanings of tea.

Additionally, integrating reminders or prompts within your Emacs setup can serve as gentle nudges to direct your attention. Creating specific commands to remind you of your intentions for each reading can anchor your mind and help eliminate distractions while engaging with the tea. For example, before each session, inputting a command that randomly selects specific themes from a list can prompt you to consider your focus for the day, guiding your interpretation toward particular aspects of life you may wish to explore.

Another beneficial feature of Emacs is the ability to avoid notifications and distractions commonly found on other digital platforms. By turning off unrelated notifications while working within Emacs, you create a sanctuary focused purely on your readings. This single-mindedness promotes a deeper immersion into the tea leaf interpretation process—allowing you to access your intuitive thoughts without the interruptive noise that often permeates our hyper-connected lives.

During actual reading sessions, consider employing a simple mindfulness technique to foster focus further. Before you begin interpreting the symbols formed by the tea leaves, take a moment to breathe deeply and settle into the present moment. Use Emacs to display calming text or visuals during your reading to evoke mindfulness and tranquility. Placing reminder phrases or symbols that resonate with calmness in your Emacs workspace may help reinforce this focus, guiding your intuitive interpretation of the tea leaves.

As you progress in your practice, experiment with various configurations or packages that enhance your focus. Emacs supports a vast array of third-party packages designed to streamline tasks, showcase visual representations of your notes, and provide automated analyses of previous readings. By continuously refining your setup, you can cultivate an environment that nurtures productivity and creativity while honoring the mystical aspects of tasseography.

In conclusion, leveraging Emacs to enhance focus during tea leaf readings transforms the practice into a structured and intentional experience. By organizing your workspace, utilizing features like Org mode, minimizing distractions, and incorporating mindfulness techniques, you cultivate an environment rich with potential for insights and reflections. The synergy between focused intention and the fluid interpretation of tea leaves creates a profound journey into self-discovery, illuminating pathways to understanding one's life and experiences through the ancient art of tasseography.

8. Guiding Principles of Self-Discovery

8.1. Journey of Inner Discovery

The journey of inner discovery through tea leaf reading offers a unique opportunity for personal growth and understanding. Tasseography, an ancient practice interwoven with symbolism, provides insights that can illuminate one's path in life. When we engage with the remnants of tea leaves left in a cup, we open ourselves to a dialogue with our subconscious, inviting interpretations that can reveal deeper truths about our emotional and spiritual states.

At its core, tea leaf reading acts as a mirror, reflecting our innermost feelings, fears, and aspirations. The shapes formed by the leaves serve as a canvas upon which we project our thoughts, creating a connection between our current experiences and the cosmic patterns that shape our lives. This process of interpretation fosters self-awareness, encouraging practitioners to explore their inner worlds and confront issues that may otherwise be suppressed. For many, this transformative practice becomes a catalyst for self-exploration, guiding them on a journey toward authenticity and alignment with their true selves.

Using Emacs as a supportive tool can further enhance this journey of inner discovery. By documenting insights and reflections in an organized manner, practitioners cultivate a habit of mindfulness and introspection. The process of writing down interpretations not only fosters clarity but also encourages one to engage steadily with the symbols encountered in their readings. Over time, these recorded insights create a narrative of personal growth, allowing patterns to emerge that highlight areas of strength and opportunities for development.

In the practice of tea leaf reading, symbols resonate with the subconscious mind, inviting readers to unearth hidden meanings and confront personal truths. This symbolic language, deeply rooted in cultural histories, offers practitioners a bridge to connect with their intuition and spiritual selves. Each reading serves as an exploration of the psyche, where shapes and forms become tangible expressions of internal experiences. In this manner, practitioners learn to trust their intuitive insights, incorporating them into their daily lives to foster greater self-understanding.

Integrating tea leaf readings into a routine can further promote self-reflection and awareness. Regular readings can serve as checkpoints in one's emotional landscape, allowing for an ongoing dialogue with oneself. By establishing dedicated times for reflection, individuals can create a sacred ritual that nurtures their growth and encourages alignment with their aspirations.

The insights gained from readings often extend beyond the cup, influencing real-world decisions and actions. As practitioners engage with the symbols, they may find clarity regarding life choices, relationships, and personal goals. Embracing the messages presented by the tea leaves prompts individuals to act with confidence and conviction, using the wisdom gleaned from their readings to inform life decisions.

Ultimately, the potential for self-discovery and growth through tea leaf reading is vast. The echoes of ancient practices resonate in modern methods, where technology and tradition intertwine to facilitate personal exploration. As practitioners embark on this journey, they are reminded that the true power lies not just in the shapes formed by the leaves but in their willingness to embrace the insights uncovered.

With each cup brewed and each reading interpreted, tea leaf readings become a canvas for self-discovery that reveals the deepest facets of one's journey—an invitation to explore and unravel the layers of the self while fostering a deep connection with the world around them. Through tea leaf reading, individuals can awaken their intuition, cultivate self-awareness, and navigate their paths with newfound clarity, ultimately illuminating their unique journeys toward enlightenment and inner peace.

8.2. Journaling with Emacs

Journaling after tea leaf readings in Emacs is a powerful way to capture insights and track personal growth over time. This process not only enhances the reflective practice of tasseography but also integrates the analytical capabilities of Emacs to create a comprehensive record of your experiences.

To begin with, it's essential to create a dedicated space within Emacs for your journaling. Utilizing the benefits of Org Mode can be particularly advantageous here. You might consider setting up an Org file specifically for tea leaf readings. This organization allows for efficient documentation with easy access to previous entries and reflections.

As you engage in each reading, take a moment to note the date, the type of tea used, and your initial thoughts about what you expect from the reading. This context is important, as it establishes a baseline for future comparisons. When you log your readings, dedicate sections to describe the symbols you observed in the leaves as well as your interpretations. Aim to capture both the objective observations—the shapes formed, how prominent they were—alongside your emotional responses and any intuitive insights that arise during the session.

Incorporating visual elements into your journaling process can further enrich your entries. For instance, you might take photographs of the tea leaves left in the cup or even sketch the symbols directly within your Emacs document. This visual representation can serve as a poignant reminder of the reading, reinforcing your interpretations when you revisit those notes later.

Another beneficial practice is to include prompts for reflection after the reading is completed. Ask yourself questions such as: What resonated most about the symbols observed? Did any of the interpretations align with recent life events or emotional states? How do these insights affect your current perspectives or actions? Documenting your responses to these questions not only deepens the practice but also helps track evolving thoughts and insights over time.

For those who may find it helpful, creating tags or keywords for each entry in your Org Mode document can streamline the process of reviewing your journey. As certain symbols recur or themes emerge, you can easily filter through your entries to observe how your interpretations have shifted or remained constant. This ability to track change provides valuable insight into your growth as a practitioner of tasseography and enhances your reflective practice.

Moreover, you might find it valuable to set aside monthly or quarterly sessions to revisit your journal and analyze trends in your readings. Reflect upon how symbols have shifted in meaning for you and consider how the insights gained have impacted your decision-making processes. This structured reflection encourages growth and fuels a deeper understanding of the interconnectedness between your tea leaf readings and life experiences.

With Emacs as your journaling platform, you have the flexibility to wander beyond simple documentation. You can integrate additional functionalities, such as creating charts to visualize the frequency of certain symbols over time or linking your readings to specific themes in your life. This dynamic approach makes your journaling process an engaging facet of your tea leaf reading practice.

Ultimately, journaling with Emacs transforms the act of tea leaf reading from a fleeting moment into a profound ongoing dialogue with yourself. By capturing your thoughts, insights, and evolving interpretations, you honor the ritual of tasseography while simultaneously fostering personal growth. This unique blend of tradition with the innovative capabilities of Emacs empowers you to explore the depths of self-discovery through the mystical journey of tea leaf reading.

8.3. Symbolic Language and Subconscious Mind

In the context of tea leaf reading, the relationship between symbolic language and the subconscious mind is both intriguing and intricate. This connection delves into how our inherent understanding and emotional responses shape the way we interpret the symbols formed by tea leaves, empowering us to extract meanings that reflect our own lives and experiences.

At the heart of this interplay lies the concept that symbols are more than mere shapes; they act as gateways to our subconscious thoughts, feelings, and desires. Each reader approaches a cup of tea with a unique life story, laden with personal associations tied to various shapes and motifs. For example, the appearance of a circle could evoke ideas of completeness or cycles in life, while a star might bring forth feelings of hope or aspirations for success based on an individual's previous encounters with such symbols.

As practitioners engage in the reading of tea leaves, they tap into their subconscious, invoking images, emotions, and memories that resonate with the symbols before them. This process transforms an arbitrary selection of shapes into a rich tapestry of meanings tailored to the querent's circumstances. In essence, the symbolic language of tea leaves incorporates layers of interpretations woven together by the reader's reflections and immediate emotional reactions. By recognizing these connections, readers gain insights not just about their surroundings but also about their own identities and inner dialogues.

The role of the subconscious in this practice cannot be understated. Often, readers may find that meanings reveal themselves through intuition rather than conscious reasoning. It is the subconscious that recognizes patterns and makes sense of symbol occurrences based on personal experiences. When engaging with tea leaves, individuals may notice symbols that stir up forgotten aspirations or remind them of past disappointments. Such connections can surface insights that are not readily accessible through rational thought alone, bringing clarity to areas of life where uncertainty prevails.

One interesting approach for readers is to maintain a detailed journal of their readings, documenting not only the symbols encountered but also the corresponding feelings and thoughts that arise during the interpretation process. This practice establishes a dialogue with the subconscious, helping individuals become more attuned to their own narratives and the symbolic meanings that resonate within them. Embracing a digital platform like Emacs for this documentation allows readers to categorize experiences easily, filter through recurring themes, and explore personal growth over time.

Particularly powerful is the ability to recognize the broader context of shared symbolism across different cultures. While certain shapes generally convey universally recognized meanings, such as a heart representing love or a snake indicating transformation, the deeper personal associations may vary widely among individuals. This diversity underscores the rich complexity of human consciousness, encouraging readers to adopt a more nuanced perspective on interpretations.

Moreover, incorporating mindfulness into the reading process strengthens the connection to the subconscious. By approaching readings with intention and focus, practitioners may discover that they are more receptive to subtle cues and insights. Practicing stillness before commencing a reading can help clear the mind of distractions, allowing a deeper connection to the symbolic language present. Engaging in meditation or breathing exercises can prime the reader's mind for this exploration, establishing a conducive mental landscape for intuitive insights to arise.

The merging of symbolic language with subconscious exploration offers practitioners a profound opportunity to not only glean insights from tea leaves but to understand their own psychological landscapes. As individuals brave this journey within themselves, they cultivate a deeper sense of self-awareness, enhancing their connection to the symbols represented.

Ultimately, the interplay between symbolic language and the subconscious in tea leaf reading creates a powerful framework for personal discovery. By embracing intuition and emotional resonance, readers unlock a wealth of insights that reflect their deeply held truths and aspirations. The leaves speak, but it is the reader's inner self that translates their stories, guiding them toward self-understanding, growth, and clarity. Engaging fully with this practice fosters an enriching dialogue that connects the mystical art of tasseography to the core of human experience, inviting us to explore the narratives shaped by both our lives and the symbols within each cup.

8.4. Promoting Self-reflection and Awareness

In the quest for self-reflection and awareness, tea leaf reading emerges as a multifaceted practice that invites individuals to delve into their inner worlds. This ancient art offers a unique opportunity to explore the subconscious through the symbolism inherent in tea leaves. Engaging with this practice encourages a dialogue between the reader and the intuitive insights emerging from the patterns formed in the bottom of the cup. The act of reading tea leaves becomes much more than mere fortune-telling; it serves as a profound means for understanding oneself and one's journey.

To begin, establishing a routine that incorporates regular tea leaf readings fosters self-awareness. By setting aside dedicated time for this practice—be it weekly, monthly, or after significant life events—individuals create a sacred ritual that allows for introspection. Within this framework, tea leaves serve as mirrors, reflecting emotions, thoughts, and even future potentials. Each reading becomes a focal point for exploration, allowing individuals to observe their evolving feelings and thoughts over time.

As the leaves settle into shapes and forms, the reader is prompted to interact with their internal landscape. This engagement encourages participants not only to seek meaning from symbols but also to look inward, allowing the practice to inspire personal revelations and growth. Mindfully interpreting the shapes fosters awareness of one's emotional states, guiding individuals toward clarity about their desires, challenges, and aspirations.

Incorporating a journaling component, particularly through tools like Emacs, enhances the reflection process. Documenting readings alongside personal insights serves to solidify the connection between the intuitive interpretations derived from the leaves and the practical aspects of one's life. Over time, this organized record becomes a valuable resource, allowing individuals to trace how their insights align with real-world experiences. By examining patterns in their readings, practitioners can identify recurring themes, uncover unresolved issues, and celebrate their personal evolution.

Using tea leaf readings as a guide for life decisions further nurtures self-awareness. The insights acquired from interpreting the leaves can illuminate various paths to navigate life's choices. By considering the messages offered by the shapes, practitioners can approach important decisions with a heightened sense of clarity. Engaging with the leaves as a tool for guidance transforms the readings into a meaningful compass, fostering confidence in making choices that resonate with one's core values and aspirations.

Moreover, the practice of tea leaf reading can evoke conversations with oneself about personal beliefs, fears, and motivations. By cultivating a non-judgmental attitude toward interpretations, practitioners may unravel layers of understanding that reveal hidden aspects of their psyche. This conversational approach encourages exploration of various dimensions within oneself, enhancing emotional intelligence and fostering a deeper connection to personal truths.

As practitioners delve deeper into their readings, the intertwining of intuition and reflection enhances their understanding of their personal narratives. The tea leaves serve as both the canvas and the brush, creating intricate portraits of individual experiences and inviting practitioners to embrace their journeys fully. Engaging with the leaves encourages a sense of empowerment, providing individuals with a framework to navigate challenges and celebrate growth based on the insights gained.

Through this ongoing practice, individuals can promote a lifestyle centered around self-reflection, encouraging continuous personal and emotional exploration. The integration of mindfulness into tea leaf reading emphasizes observation over judgment, cultivating a space where insights can flourish freely. As readers consistently engage with their practice, they unveil the potential hidden within each cup, leading to a transformative journey towards greater self-awareness and connection to the patterns that shape their lives.

In summary, incorporating tea leaf reading into a routine can significantly enhance one's capacity for self-reflection and awareness. The practice encourages individuals to engage deeply with the symbolism present in the leaves, fostering a connection between intuitive insights and personal growth. By documenting interpretations in a structured format using tools like Emacs, practitioners can create a rich tapestry of experiences that illuminate their journeys. Ultimately, tea leaf reading invites individuals to explore their inner landscapes, promoting self-awareness and understanding as they navigate the complexities of life through the wisdom reflected in their tea leaves.

8.5. Using Readings to Inform Life Decisions

Using tea leaf readings to inform life decisions involves a nuanced process that intertwines intuition, insight, and practical application. As practitioners delve into this ancient art, they may discover profound revelations that guide their choices and shape their personal journeys. The interplay of symbols formed by tea leaves creates a rich tapestry of meaning, and by learning to interpret these messages effectively, readers can empower themselves in their decision-making processes.

To begin, it's essential to engage with the symbolism of the tea leaves as a tool for reflection. Each reading serves as a snapshot of one's current emotional landscape, revealing underlying desires, concerns, and aspirations. The practice of tea leaf reading enables individuals to not only uncover their subconscious inclinations but also to confront areas of their lives needing attention or change. Therefore, approaching readings with mindfulness and intention allows practitioners to gain clarity on specific decisions they may be grappling with—be it in relationships, career paths, or personal growth.

When interpreting the shapes formed by tea leaves, practitioners should consider their emotional responses to these symbols. For example, a heart-shaped formation might resonate with feelings of love or connection, prompting the querent to reflect on their current relationships and whether they align with their desires. Similarly, a key shape may symbolize new opportunities; in this instance, it could urge the individual to weigh their options regarding career changes or educational pursuits. Thus, the insights gained from the shapes can inform important life decisions and encourage proactive thinking.

Practitioners can enhance their decision-making process by drawing direct connections between their readings and real-world contexts. After documenting the interpretations, they can pose reflective questions related to the reading. Questions may center around themes such as: How do the symbols relate to my current situation? Are there patterns emerging that indicate a path I should follow? What actions can I take based on these insights? By objectively analyzing these relationships, individuals may uncover actionable guidance from the tea leaves, translating symbolism into tangible steps.

Moreover, utilizing technology—such as Emacs for documenting and analyzing readings—facilitates an organized approach to monitoring decisions influenced by tea leaf interpretations. By maintaining a record of past readings alongside the decisions made based on those insights, practitioners can assess the outcomes and learn from their experiences over time. This iterative process not only tracks growth but also reinforces the value of the insights gained through the tea leaves.

Incorporating community feedback can further enhance this reflective practice. Engaging with fellow practitioners provides valuable perspectives and suggestions that can inform decision-making. Sharing readings in workshops or online communities enables individuals to gain insights from others' interpretations, allowing them to see their situations from different viewpoints. This collaborative aspect fosters a sense of belonging and support, enhancing the reading experience while empowering each reader to take informed action in their lives.

However, it's essential to maintain a balanced perspective regarding the role of tea leaf readings in decision-making. While insights can be illuminating, one must remember that readings should complement, rather than rely solely upon, logical reasoning and practical considerations. Readers must discern when to trust the messages from the leaves and when to weigh them against the realities of their circumstances. Recognizing this balance fosters a thoughtful approach to interpreting symbols, ensuring decisions are made with clarity and a grounded understanding of one's goals.

Lastly, practitioners should embrace flexibility in their reading practice. Life is fluid, and as new experiences unfold, the relevance of specific insights may change. Engaging in repeat readings over time can provide updated perspectives on ongoing situations, allowing individuals to adapt their decisions based on evolving insights. By cultivating a continual dialogue with the tea leaves, readers remain aligned with their intuition and navigate life's complexities with confidence.

In summary, using tea leaf readings to inform life decisions involves a harmonious blend of introspection, reflection, and proactive engagement. By interpreting the symbols formed by the leaves, documenting insights effectively, and remaining open to both intuition and rationality, practitioners can empower themselves in their decision-making processes. Ultimately, tea leaf readings serve as a guiding light, illuminating paths to clarity, purpose, and self-discovery in the journey of life.

9. Decoding the Future: The Mystical and the Practical

9.1. Prophecies in Tea: Fact or Fiction?

In the world of tea leaf reading, the question of whether prophecies obtained from this ancient practice are fact or fiction becomes compelling. Tasseography, the art of interpreting the patterns formed by tea leaves, has captivated the imaginations of many, sparking discussions on the validity of its insights. As a bridge between the mystical and the analytical, this practice invites practitioners and skeptics alike to navigate the intricacies of divination versus mere chance.

First, it is essential to recognize the underlying belief system that informs tea leaf reading. Many practitioners approach this ancient art with a sense of reverence, adhering to the notion that tea leaves hold the potential to reveal profound truths about one's life path, relationships, and surroundings. The interpretation of shapes and symbols created by settled leaves is thought to facilitate a dialogue between the reader, their intuition, and external circumstances. This perspective embraces the idea that the universe communicates through signs, urging individuals to listen closely to glean the wisdom embedded in their readings.

On the flip side of this belief lies skepticism—a viewpoint that questions the legitimacy of tea leaf readings as prophetic. Critics argue that the interpretations drawn from tea leaves are subjective, reliant on personal intuition, and influenced by cognitive biases. They posit that these readings often lack empirical evidence, viewing the process as an exercise in pattern recognition rather than divination. This perspective suggests that individuals might be reading into the symbolism what they wish or expect to find, rather than uncovering objective truths.

Navigating the intersection of these two perspectives—belief and skepticism—requires a thoughtful approach. Practitioners of tea leaf reading must recognize that their interpretations can be influenced by their emotions, biases, and life experiences. The shapes formed by the leaves may resonate with specific meanings based on individual circumstances, but they do not guarantee predetermined outcomes. Readers are encouraged to balance their intuitive insights with a grounded sense of self-awareness, ensuring they remain open to the messages in the tea leaves without devolving into wishful thinking.

For many, the true power of tea leaf reading lies in its capacity to foster self-reflection rather than predict the future. The leaves can serve as a catalyst for contemplation, guiding readers to explore their emotions, struggles, and aspirations. The insights gained may resonate on a personal level, inspiring individuals to examine their choices and behaviors, ultimately empowering them to take charge of their destinies. In this sense, the prophecies in tea may not be literal predictions but rather invitations to engage more deeply with one's life.

Moreover, the experience of engaging with tea leaves can foster a sense of community and connection among practitioners. As readers gather around a table to enjoy tea, they create shared moments where insights are exchanged, and interpretations are discussed. This communal aspect enhances the practice's richness, allowing collaborative exploration of meanings that might resonate with multiple individuals simultaneously. The resulting dialogue contributes to a collective understanding of the symbols, emphasizing that tea leaf reading can cultivate more than just individual interpretations; it can also facilitate connections, empathy, and support.

As technology merges into the practice, the dynamics of skepticism and belief continue to evolve. Digital platforms allow for the sharing of readings, interpretations, and techniques among communities around the world. While some may still question the authenticity of tea leaf readings, others embrace the practice as a valuable exploratory tool. Software like Emacs not only aids in documenting insights but also facilitates communication and collaboration among practitioners, helping to demystify tea leaf readings for newcomers and skeptics alike.

Ultimately, the truth behind the prophecies in tea may be less about whether they constitute crystal-clear truths and more about the meaning that individuals derive from them. The experience of tea leaf reading becomes a personal journey of introspection, connections, and growth. By encouraging a balanced perspective—one that recognizes the art's mystical allure while contemplating the role of personal interpretation—readers can navigate the enigmatic world of tasseography with greater awareness.

In conclusion, while prophecies arising from tea leaf readings may be viewed through a lens of skepticism or belief, understanding the context of the practice is crucial. The essence of tasseography lies in fostering self-reflection, enhancing connections with others, and promoting growth along one's unique path. As readers engage with this captivating form of divination, they are invited to embrace a journey where the boundaries between fact and fiction converge in the delicate dance of tea leaves—an invitation to explore their own truths with curiosity and openness.

9.2. Recognizing True Revelations

The practice of recognizing true revelations within the context of tea leaf reading involves navigating the space between structured interpretations and intuitive insights. Tasseography, with its rich tradition and deeply personal nature, invites practitioners to explore the shapes formed by tea leaves left behind in a cup. However, not all readings yield profound insights; thus, developing the skill to discern valuable revelations from inconclusive interpretations is essential for enhancing the practice.

To embark on this journey, practitioners first need to establish a clear mindset before engaging in a reading. With an open heart and readiness to receive insights, individuals can set intentions that guide their interpretations. This preparatory phase serves as a grounding mechanism, allowing practitioners to contextualize their readings and approach the shapes formed by the leaves with an inquisitive spirit. By discarding preconceived notions and being willing to embrace the unknown, practitioners are better positioned to recognize authentic revelations hidden within the symbols.

As tea leaves settle, practitioners can begin their thoughtful observation of the shapes. Important shapes and symbols often emerge, suggesting connections to specific areas of life. Nonetheless, it is crucial for readers to reflect upon the emotional context attached to these symbols. True revelations resonate deeply within one's experiences and emotions, while inconclusive shapes may lack that connection, leaving the reader feeling detached. Hence, taking note of which shapes elicit strong emotional responses or personal resonance offers valuable insights.

Moreover, maintaining a journal of readings—potentially structured within a tool such as Emacs—helps readers review past interpretations. This practice fosters a reflective process whereby individuals can revisit their readings and gauge the impact of previous insights on their experiences. Patterns might emerge over time that inform the reader of symbols that resonate with them beyond a singular reading. This retrospect encourages a deeper understanding of how true revelations can manifest consistently throughout one's life.

Practical criteria can also assist readers in evaluating the significance of interpretations. True revelations often carry a sense of clarity and alignment with one's life narrative, guiding the reader toward actionable steps or new perspectives. In contrast, inconclusive readings may feel vague or stir confusion without a clear directive. Learning to differentiate between these responses allows practitioners to cultivate the skill of intuition, ultimately leading to deeper insights rooted in personal authenticity.

An openness to continuous learning also enriches the practice of recognizing true revelations. Engaging with communities of fellow practitioners provides opportunities to share experiences and interpretations, enhancing each individual's understanding of the symbols. The collective wisdom garnered from diverse perspectives not only sharpens interpretation skills but may also highlight over-looked aspects that contribute to identifying meaningful insights.

Finally, it's essential to balance realistic expectations with the mystical properties inherent in tea leaf readings. While the practice invites intuition, it does not guarantee absolute clarity or prophetic outcomes. Encouraging readers to retain a healthy skepticism allows them to approach their readings with thoughtful discernment, recognizing that true revelations unfold with time and reflection rather than instant clarity. By fostering a mindset that appreciates the journey rather than solely the destination, practitioners are likely to experience a more authentic connection to the practice.

In conclusion, the journey of recognizing true revelations in tea leaf reading is multifaceted, encompassing intentional observation, emotional connection, retrospective analysis, and community engagement. By embracing a reflective and open-minded approach, practitioners can navigate the intricate dance between intuitive insights and structured interpretations, ultimately enhancing the depth and significance of their readings. As tea leaves whisper their secrets, it is through mindful interpretation that the true revelations emerge, illuminating the pathways ahead with clarity and understanding.

9.3. Balancing Expectations with Reality

The interplay between expectations and the realities of tea leaf reading can often create a complex landscape. For many enthusiasts, the allure of tasseography lies in its promise of insight into the future —a tantalizing glimpse into what might be. However, the delicate balance between these anticipations and the truths revealed through the reading process is crucial for both personal growth and the effectiveness of the practice.

When embarking on a tea leaf reading, it's natural to carry a set of expectations influenced by previous experiences, prevailing cultural narratives, or specific desires for clarity in decision-making. Readers may hope for prophetic insights pertaining to love, career choices, or personal fulfillment. However, it's essential to recognize that interpreting tea leaves is less about yielding definitive predictions and more about reflecting on the present, understanding one's self, and discovering pathways for growth.

One common pitfall arises when individuals approach readings with rigid expectations. When a reading fails to align with what they hoped to discover, disappointment can quickly set in, causing them to question the legitimacy of the symbols or, worse, their abilities as readers. This disconnect between anticipation and reality warrants a flexible mindset that allows for adaptability and openness to the wisdom that emerges—not merely focusing on their desired outcomes but considering what the symbols may reveal about their current emotional landscape and life context.

The essence of tea leaf reading lies in its symbolic nature. Each shape formed by the remnants of tea is open to interpretation, contingent not only upon traditional meanings but also upon the reader's intuition, emotions, and personal experiences. A heart could signify romantic love, or it could represent self-love; a key might unlock new opportunities or might signify a need to access hidden insights within oneself. Recognizing that these symbols can convey multiple meanings allows for a richer dialogue with the reading, nurturing a broader understanding and enhancing the reading's relevance in the reader's life.

To anchor one's practice in reality, it is vital to cultivate reflective habits that embrace both the subjective and objective elements of readings. Practitioners can enhance their experiences by documenting their readings in detail, considering not just the shapes formed but also accompanying emotions and thoughts. Engaging with technology, such as utilizing Emacs to organize readings, can facilitate a continuous dialogue around evolving interpretations.

Moreover, fostering a sense of community encourages practitioners to share their thoughts and insights, creating a network of support that normalizes the spectrum of outcomes a reading can yield. In discussing various interpretations with fellow readers, individuals can learn to appreciate the diversity of perspectives within tasseography, which can help recalibrate any unmet expectations. Engaging in a shared narrative around the reading experience nurtures growth and fosters understanding that the journey of tea leaf reading is as valuable as the destination.

Setting personal intentions for each reading can create a grounding framework that clarifies one's desires without imposing rigid expectations. Structuring these intentions as open-ended statements invites a more fluid engagement with the symbols. Statements like, "What guidance can I glean from this reading?" or "What insights might the leaves reveal about my current challenges?" help frame the reading in a way that acknowledges the present moment, heightens awareness of unfolding themes, and nurtures curiosity.

Finally, patience and acceptance play integral roles in balancing expectations with reality in tea leaf reading. Embracing the unfolding nature of life, along with the organic pace of intuitive insights, allows practitioners to cultivate a greater sense of trust in the process. Each reading can be viewed as a step along the path, where the richness of the insights derives from the exploration rather than merely the outcomes.

As practitioners navigate the dance between expectation and reality, tea leaf readings become powerful tools for self-discovery. By maintaining a flexible mindset, documenting insights, fostering community engagement, and cultivating patience, readers not only uncover the wisdom embedded in the leaves but also embark on an enriching personal journey of meaning and growth.

9.4. Practical Applications of Tasseography in Daily Life

In the enchanting practice of tasseography, tea leaf reading transcends mere divining; it becomes a powerful tool for self-discovery and practical application in daily life. The art of interpreting tea leaves connects ancient wisdom with modern insights, offering practitioners profound revelations that can guide both personal and professional decisions. By harnessing the symbolism inherent in tea leaves, readers can navigate their life choices, evaluate their paths, and foster a sense of clarity and purpose.

To begin with, the key to utilizing readings effectively lies in establishing a clear intention prior to sipping your cup of tea. By focusing your mind on specific questions or areas of concern, you create a framework for interpretation that enhances the overall meaning derived from the shapes left behind in the cup. This intentionality acts as a guiding framework for it enables the leaves to become mirrors reflecting your innermost thoughts and feelings, rather than vague symbols devoid of relevance.

Once the tea has settled, practitioners begin the process of interpretation. The shapes that emerge hold unique meanings and often reflect the querent's current life situation. For instance, if a heart shape appears, it might represent emotional connections and relationships in the querent's life; if it's an anchor shape, it could symbolize stability, security, or the need to stay grounded in turbulent times. Understanding common symbols allows the practitioner to navigate readings effectively, using the established lore to shed light on their life experiences.

As interpretations take shape, readers must remain open to weaving their personal experiences into the meanings derived from the symbols. Acknowledging the emotional resonance of shapes cultivates a richer understanding of the insights gleaned from the leaves. This practice transforms readings from mere observations into deeply personal reflections, urging individuals to consider how the messages align with their lived realities, challenges, and aspirations.

Additionally, utilizing technology, such as Emacs for documenting readings, enhances the ability to inform decisions based on past experiences. By recording insights and reflections consistently, practitioners can analyze patterns over time, tracking how particular symbols may tie into recurring themes in their lives. This ongoing record enables one to assess the significance of tea leaf readings regarding real-life situations—be it relationship dynamics, career decisions, or self-discovery pursuits.

When faced with major life decisions, practitioners can turn to the insights derived from recent readings to inform their pathways. Whether contemplating a career change, navigating a tumultuous relationship, or embarking on a new venture, the symbols in the tea leaves often hold guidance that aligns with the reader's desires. Engaging deeply with the insights allows individuals to approach these decisions with a blend of intuition and informed reasoning, lending confidence as they take action.

Furthermore, the community surrounding tea leaf reading fosters a sense of connection and support when applying readings to life decisions. Engaging in discussions with fellow practitioners offers diverse perspectives and insights that can broaden one's understanding of symbolic meanings. Sharing experiences can reveal the subtle nuances inherent in interpreting tea leaves, enriching the learning process for all involved.

Ultimately, the practice of tea leaf reading serves as a powerful conduit for self-reflection and growth. By weaving their personal narratives into the interpretations, practitioners transform the readings into actionable insights for daily life. As they cultivate the ability to navigate decisions guided by the wisdom found within their cups, individuals embrace tea leaf reading as a transformative practice that deepens their connection to themselves and the world around them.

In summary, practical applications of tasseography in everyday life open pathways for personal transformation. By engaging thoughtfully with the symbolic meanings of tea leaves, utilizing technology for documentation, and fostering community support, practitioners can harness the reading's insights to inform critical decisions. This harmonious balance of reflection and action empowers individuals to navigate life's complexities, fostering a profound sense of self-awareness and purpose along the journey. Every reading beckons an invitation to explore, grow, and connect with the deeper truths illuminated by the enchanting dance of tea leaves.

9.5. The Ethical Responsibilities of a Reader

In the practice of tasseography, or tea leaf reading, the ethical responsibilities of a reader are essential to ensure a respectful and constructive experience for both the reader and the querent. This chapter delves into the responsibilities that come with this unique form of divination, touching upon key principles that practitioners should adhere to, promoting a positive practice steeped in respect, integrity, and understanding.

First and foremost, it is imperative for readers to foster a sense of ethical integrity in their practice. This involves approaching the interpretative process with honesty and transparency. Readers should clearly communicate the nature of tea leaf readings, setting realistic expectations for the querent and emphasizing that tea leaves serve as a tool to explore possible insights rather than definitive outcomes. By clarifying that readings are subjective and often open to interpretation, practitioners allow space for personal reflection and agency, removing any undue pressure from the experience.

Confidentiality is also a fundamental ethical responsibility. Each reading may touch on deeply personal matters, and it is the reader's duty to honor the privacy of the querent's insights. Practitioners must avoid sharing details of readings with others without explicit permission, fostering a secure environment where querents feel comfortable expressing themselves openly. This sense of safety reinforces trust between the reader and the querent, encouraging genuine engagement with the interpretation process.

Moreover, ethical readers are expected to consider the emotional impact of their interpretations. The symbols represented by tea leaves can evoke strong feelings, and the way in which insights are conveyed can significantly influence the querent's emotional state. Practitioners should approach sensitive topics with care, employing a compassionate tone and offering support rather than fear. This mindful approach ensures that the process has a beneficial effect, empowering the querent rather than unsettling them.

Additionally, tea leaf readers should be aware of their own limitations. While they may possess innate abilities to interpret symbols, it is essential to recognize when to refrain from offering advice that exceeds their expertise. For instance, sensitive topics concerning mental health, legal issues, or life and death decisions should be navigated carefully, and practitioners should direct querents to seek professional guidance when necessary. Acknowledging the boundaries of one's interpretations affirms the reader's ethical responsibility to prioritize the well-being of the querent.

Cultural sensitivity further enriches the ethical practice of tasseography. Given the diverse global tapestry of tea-drinking traditions and symbols, practitioners must honor the cultural contexts from which these practices arise. Recognizing and respecting the significance of tea leaves and their interpretations across different cultures fosters inclusive practices and promotes mutual understanding among readers and querents. By engaging thoughtfully with the cultural heritage involved in tea leaf reading, practitioners embed their work within a broader context that promotes respect and appreciation for tradition.

Moreover, mentoring and supporting fellow practitioners enhance the ethical landscape of tea leaf reading. By fostering connections within the community, experienced readers can share insights, best practices, and ethical considerations with newcomers, creating a framework of guidance that benefits the collective growth of the practice. This collaborative spirit encourages a culture of learning, where ethical standards are continually reinforced.

As practitioners navigate the complexities of ethical responsibilities within tasseography, regular self-reflection becomes an invaluable tool. Readers should engage in ongoing introspection about their motives, interpretations, and experiences throughout their practices. This reflective practice nurtures a sense of awareness about the influence they wield in the lives of others while ensuring that their readings remain rooted in integrity and accuracy. By evaluating past readings and identifying areas for growth, practitioners can enhance their focus within the ethical terrain of tea leaf reading.

In conclusion, the ethical responsibilities of a tea leaf reader encompass honesty, confidentiality, emotional sensitivity, recognition of limits, cultural appreciation, and a commitment to community growth. Through these guiding principles, practitioners can create enriching, respectful environments for their querents, promoting meaningful engagement while fostering personal development. It is by embracing these responsibilities that tea leaf readers can navigate the mystical art of tasseography with integrity and compassion, unlocking insights that catalyze transformation and self-awareness in all who embark on this journey.

10. Embracing Community and Connection

10.1. The Importance of Community in Divination

The practice of tea leaf reading, or tasseography, thrives on the importance of community and connection, emphasizing the collaborative nature of divination. Within this intricate tapestry, the shared experiences of practitioners not only deepen individual interpretations but also foster collective learning and understanding. Amid the rich cultural heritage tied to tea leaf reading, community engagement becomes a vital component—bridging the gap between traditional practices and modern expressions, and facilitating connection among those seeking insight.

In the world of tea leaf reading, shared experiences become a source of inspiration and validation. As practitioners gather, they create a supportive network that enhances each reader's understanding of the symbols and their meanings. The process of discussing readings with others allows practitioners to view interpretations from diverse perspectives. This opportunity for collective analysis enriches the reading experience, helping individuals to solidify their interpretations while opening them to new ideas and interpretations they may not have previously considered.

Using Emacs as a collaborative tool enhances this community-driven practice. Emacs can serve as a platform for note-sharing and debate, allowing users to document their individual readings while providing a space for fellow practitioners to review, comment, and build on their insights. Readers can create shared documents, integrating their interpretations and allowing for realtime contributions. This collaborative technique fosters a sense of camaraderie and encourages deeper exploration into the meanings derived from tea leaves.

Workshops and community gatherings also play a pivotal role in tea leaf reading, harnessing the collective wisdom found within group interactions. These events provide a rich environment for practitioners to share experiences and hone their skills together. Group readings allow for vivid comparisons of interpretations, revealing how various individuals can connect with the same symbols in distinct ways. This shared practice cultivates a heightened understanding of the subtleties within tasseography, offering participants new dimensions of insight into their readings.

The relational aspect of community also encourages personal growth. Engaging with those on similar journeys fosters an appreciation for the transformative potential of tea leaf reading while cultivating a sense of belonging. These interactions elevate the experience, transforming solitary readings into communal explorations of meaning. The emotional support derived from discussing personal insights with others emphasizes the value of shared narratives—offering guidance and encouragement as practitioners navigate their paths to self-discovery.

The rise of digital communities presents additional opportunities for connecting with fellow tea leaf enthusiasts. Online forums, social media groups, and dedicated websites for tasseography can unite practitioners from various backgrounds and locations. This virtual connectivity allows readers to share their insights, techniques, and experiences while enhancing the accessibility of the practice to new audiences. Digital communities not only celebrate diverse interpretations but also enable members to discuss their beliefs, explore techniques, and respond to one another's readings in real-time—creating an enriching dialogue around tea leaf interpretations.

Sharing insights and learning from one another within a community setting promotes a dynamic learning environment, nurturing both seasoned readers and newcomers alike. This exchange of knowledge can involve detailed discussions on specific symbols, guided workshops focusing on particular aspects of tea leaf reading, or collaborative projects exploring the intersection of technology and divination. As communities nurture innovation, they encourage the evolution of practices that remain respectful of tradition while embracing contemporary perspectives—a synthesis that enhances individual and collective insights.

In conclusion, embracing the significance of community and connection in tea leaf reading facilitates a deeper understanding of the practice. Collective experiences enrich individual insights, while digital technologies and collaborative techniques enable practitioners to share their journeys and interpretations with a broader audience. The communal nature of tasseography not only enhances personal readings but also fosters a vibrant dialogue where curiosity, exploration, and shared wisdom thrive. Engaging with a community of tea leaf readers promises to deepen one's connection to the ancient art form while inviting a wealth of new interpretations and opportunities for growth.

10.2. Collaborative Techniques in Emacs

In the context of Emacs, a text editor revered for its extensibility and power, collaborative techniques offer practitioners a way to enhance their tea leaf reading experience through shared insights and community engagement. Emacs serves as a flexible platform that can empower readers to document their readings, exchange interpretations, and explore the art of tasseography collectively.

One of the primary ways to facilitate collaboration within Emacs is by utilizing its robust documentation capabilities. By creating shared files or using a centralized Org mode document, multiple practitioners can contribute their interpretations and experiences of readings in a structured and organized manner. This allows the collective expression of insights to become easily accessible, fostering a sense of community as readers can reference, comment on, and learn from each other's practices.

Implementing collaborative techniques in Emacs can also extend to creating reading groups or workshops where practitioners gather both virtually and in-person. By sharing their unique setups and configurations utilized in their readings, individuals enhance their community's knowledge and skills. This sharing environment can include tutorials crafted within Emacs, guiding new practitioners on how to interpret the shapes formed by the leaves or how to maintain a digital journal. Such collaborative learning reinforces the concept that tea leaf reading is not a solitary endeavor but one enriched by collective experiences and shared wisdom.

Importantly, Emacs can facilitate discussions about symbolism and its meanings through its discussion features. Readers can engage in dialogues within the buffer, allowing for real-time exchanges of thoughts while conducting group readings. Emacs' markdown capabilities enable readers to format important notes and observations, which can then be compiled into guides or shared resources that reflect the group's collective interpretations of tea leaf readings.

Furthermore, community-driven projects can arise through collaborative efforts in Emacs. Readers may come together to develop and expand a lexicon of symbols associated with tea leaf reading. By pooling their knowledge and resources, they can curate a comprehensive dictionary that not only covers traditional meanings but also integrates personal interpretations and insights gained from various practitioners' experiences. This communal lexicon can serve as a substantial resource for both novice and experienced readers, enhancing their engagement with the practice.

As technology continues to evolve, the spirit of collaboration within the Emacs ecosystem can extend to exploring integrations with online platforms such as GitHub, where practitioners can maintain version-controlled documents of their readings and insights. This fosters an environment where the evolution of interpretations can be documented, facilitating a dialogue about how readings change and how practitioners grow over time.

Moreover, with remote learning becoming increasingly prevalent, virtual workshops that utilize Emacs for collective integrations can encourage a global exchange of teachings drawn from diverse cultural interpretations of tea leaves. Readers can share historical contexts, personal stories, and varied techniques, thereby fostering a rich tapestry of knowledge within the community.

Through these collaborative techniques, practitioners of tasseography can enhance their readings while embracing a collective spirit.

As Emacs acts as the canvas for this communal journey, individuals begin to recognize the profound power of shared learning, resulting in a vibrant environment enriched with insights, creativity, and connection.

In conclusion, the integration of collaborative techniques in Emacs offers tea leaf readers an enriching approach to their practice. By leveraging the platform's customizable features, engaging in community discussions, and sharing insights and resources, practitioners create a dynamic landscape in which both tradition and innovation coexist harmoniously, reinforcing the personal and collective nature of tasseography. Embracing collaboration not only elevates individual readings but also ignites a shared passion for exploration, growth, and the art of interpreting the whispers hidden within tea leaves.

10.3. Workshops and Groups: A Collective Wisdom

In the rich tapestry of tasseography, workshops and group readings emerge as vibrant threads weaving together individual insights and collective wisdom. The practice of tea leaf reading thrives not only in solitary reflection but also flourishes within communal settings, where shared experiences enhance the richness of interpretation and foster a deeper understanding of the symbols contained within the leaves. Engaging in group settings expands the horizons of the traditional practice, providing unique opportunities for collaboration, growth, and connection.

Workshops dedicated to tea leaf reading create an inviting space for enthusiasts—novices and seasoned practitioners alike—to come together and explore the art of tasseography collaboratively. These gatherings serve as platforms for shared learning, where participants can exchange insights, discuss interpretations, and navigate the complexities of reading tea leaves together. In a structured environment, readers can practice their skills while benefiting from the diverse perspectives offered by fellow learners.

The communal aspect of workshops encourages open dialogue about the symbols present in the tea leaves. Each participant brings their own experiences, personal resonances, and emotional associations to the collective reading. What one person sees as a symbol of love might resonate differently for another, highlighting the layered meanings that emerge from interpretations. Such exchanges foster an enriched understanding, allowing practitioners to observe how the same shapes are perceived through varied lenses. This dynamic of interpretations broadens the interpretations available to everyone involved, enhancing the individual reader's journey through a shared exploration of the leaves.

Facilitators of workshops play an essential role in nurturing a supportive environment for learning. They guide participants through various techniques, helping them to develop both their analytical and intuitive skills. Interactive exercises, discussions on symbolism, and hands-on practice with real-time readings create an immersive experience that encourages participants to embrace their unique reading styles while honing their craft.

Group readings also promote the notion of connection within the tea leaf reading community. When individuals come together to read the same cup of tea, they unlock a shared narrative, converging their respective interpretations into one multifaceted story. This collective storytelling fosters deeper ties among participants, creating an inviting atmosphere for camaraderie and support. As readers engage in conversations about their insights, they cultivate bonds that can extend beyond the reading itself—nurturing a sense of belonging and encouragement among fellow practitioners.

Digital communities also supplement the benefits of in-person workshops, offering a platform for practitioners to connect regardless of geographical limitations. Online forums and social media groups focused on tea leaf reading facilitate the sharing of experiences and interpretations in real time. These virtual spaces empower individuals to ask questions, seek guidance, and exchange insights, fortifying a global community of tea leaf enthusiasts dedicated to the craft. The ease of connecting with others who share similar interests encourages continuous learning and exploration—where insights and revelations can be experienced and shared widely.

As tea leaf reading continues to evolve, the integration of innovative digital tools enhances the community experience. Beyond in-person gatherings, webinars and virtual workshops allow practitioners to connect in real-time, expanding the reach of knowledge-sharing opportunities. Utilizing software tools such as Emacs can provide structured methods for documenting group readings and discussions, enabling practitioners to collectively reflect on their insights over time. This merging of tradition and technology offers a unique approach to group interpretations, guiding practitioners towards deeper layers of understanding within their readings.

Ultimately, workshops and group readings embody the spirit of collective wisdom within tea leaf reading. By fostering environments where practitioners can come together to share insights, practice skills, and explore the multifaceted nature of interpretations, these gatherings enrich the reading experience immeasurably. Participants emerge not only with personal insights but also with a sense of connectedness—strengthening the bonds among readers and honoring the ancient art of tasseography through a shared journey of discovery. As tea leaf readers embrace the collective wisdom available through workshops and groups, they cultivate a vibrant community that nurtures creativity, inquiry, and a deep reverence for the guidance revealed through the tea leaves.

10.4. Sharing Insights and Learnings

Sharing insights and learnings in the context of tea leaf reading, or tasseography, plays a pivotal role in enhancing the practice for both seasoned readers and newcomers. This sharing transcends mere knowledge transfer; it embodies the growth of a community bound together by a mutual appreciation for the art of interpreting tea leaves. Engaging with fellow practitioners allows individuals to explore a rich landscape of interpretations, experiences, and techniques fostering collective wisdom.

One of the most enriching aspects of sharing insights is the opportunity for collaborative learning. Practitioners of tasseography often develop interpretations based on personal experiences, traditions, and cultural backgrounds. When individuals come together, they introduce diverse perspectives that can illuminate meanings previously overlooked. For instance, examining a symbol like a heart in a reading may resonate differently for someone experiencing romantic love compared to another reflecting on self-love or familial bonds. These varied interpretations enhance the depth of understanding each participant brings to their readings.

Moreover, group discussions or workshops centered around tea leaf reading create an inviting atmosphere where participants can share their journeys, observations, and interpretations. These collaborative settings encourage open dialogue, facilitating a space where questions can be posed without fear of judgment. As readers engage in collective interpretation, they refine their skills, explore new contexts, and deepen relationships with both their practice and each other. Workshops provide an opportunity to engage in hands-on practice, where role-playing and sharing readings can enrich the community's skill set.

Digital platforms further enhance the ability to share insights within the tea leaf reading community. Online forums, social media groups, and platforms like Emacs provide a medium for practitioners to exchange ideas, experiences, and resources across geographic boundaries. By connecting with others passionate about tasseography, individuals can access a wealth of information, dive into discussions on interpretative techniques, and collaborate on projects exploring the integration of tea leaf reading with technology. This exchange reinforces a sense of belonging and kinship, showcasing that one is part of a larger pursuit of knowledge and understanding.

The act of sharing insights also promotes self-reflection. As practitioners articulate their interpretations and discuss their readings with others, they engage in reflective processes that can reveal underlying motivations and beliefs. This reciprocal exchange deepens self-awareness and helps individuals recognize patterns in their readings, affirming their intuitive capabilities. The conversations that arise from sharing provide an opportunity for practitioners to challenge their assumptions, broaden their perspectives, and solidify their roles as part of the tapestry that is the tea leaf reading community.

Additionally, organizing collaborative projects within the community can provide a structured outlet for sharing insights. This could involve creating a communal symbol dictionary that encapsulates interpretations, experiences, and meanings associated with various shapes. Such a resource not only serves as a reference for individual practitioners but becomes a collective contribution to the wider community. This unity fosters an atmosphere of shared growth where knowledge can continuously evolve.

Moreover, the narratives that emerge through shared experiences can become symbolic tales connecting the collective journey of tea leaf reading practitioners. Each reader's interpretation contributes to a broader understanding of the art, showcasing how the practice transcends personal boundaries and speaks to universal human experiences. By weaving these stories together, the community nurtures its identity, capturing the essence of tea leaf reading as a living tradition.

In conclusion, sharing insights and learnings within the context of tea leaf reading serves as a powerful catalyst for individual growth and community connection. Through collaborative exchanges, reflective practices, and the embrace of diverse perspectives, practitioners cultivate a rich tapestry of understanding that enhances their engagement with tasseography. As the community grows through these shared experiences, tea leaf reading continues to evolve, blending tradition with innovation, curiosity, and creativity—inviting all involved to explore the depths of meaning waiting within each cup.

10.5. Digital Communities and Resources

In the world of modern fortune-telling, particularly within the sphere of tasseography, digital communities and resources have emerged as catalytic forces in the practice and understanding of this ancient art. Just as tea leaf reading connects individuals with rich histories and cultural narratives, the advent of technology and the internet has transformed the way practitioners engage with this mystical tool. This subchapter explores the significance of digital platforms, community engagement, and accessible resources that inspire a resurgence of interest in tea leaf reading, making it more accessible, collaborative, and reflective of our digital age.

The rise of online forums, social media groups, and dedicated websites for tea leaf reading has forged a diverse community of enthusiasts, practitioners, and newcomers. These digital spaces encourage practitioners to share experiences, readings, and interpretations, creating a vibrant tapestry of collective knowledge. The unique aspect of digital communities lies in their ability to transcend geographical boundaries, allowing individuals worldwide to connect, discuss, and collaborate in their passion for tasseography. This newfound interconnectedness elevates the practice as it draws upon global traditions and experiences, enhancing the richness of readings.

Forums and discussion groups focused on tea leaf reading offer invaluable platforms for sharing insights and exploring the nuances of interpretation. Practitioners can turn to these spaces to ask questions, exchange best practices, and participate in discussions surrounding the symbolism of tea leaves. By actively engaging in community conversations, readers can expand their understanding of various interpretations and develop their intuitive skills in new and exciting ways. This collective wisdom often reinforces the significance of different symbols while allowing for personalized interpretations shaped by individual experiences.

Moreover, social media platforms provide a contemporary venue for practitioners to showcase their readings creatively. Instagram, for example, has become a visual diary for many tea leaf readers, where they post images of their readings accompanied by narratives that unravel the meanings derived from the leaves. This interactive format not only celebrates individual interpretations but also invites conversations around those experiences, fostering a sense of belonging among practitioners. As readers witness the diverse applications of tea leaf interpretations, they are encouraged to see the beauty in difference and adapt their approaches accordingly.

In conjunction with collaborative platforms, online tutorials, and educational resources have sprung up, guiding practitioners in developing their skills. Video content, webinars, and written guides provide insights into the theory and practice of tasseography from various perspectives, teaching individuals the art of interpreting symbols and engaging with their own journeys through readings. These resources deepen the practical knowledge of readers, allowing them to refine their abilities and explore the extensive language of tea leaves more confidently.

Digital tools also enhance the recording process associated with tea leaf readings. Platforms like Emacs allow practitioners to maintain organized notes, categorize symbols, and track personal journeys over time. Utilizing Emacs not only structurally supports readers but also facilitates a deeper reflective process, encouraging them to examine their individual narratives through the lens of tea leaves. The synergy between technology and traditional practices creates a harmonious environment for experimentation and growth.

Finally, the availability of digital resources democratizes tasseography, allowing individuals from diverse backgrounds and experiences to engage with this ancient practice. Accessibility promotes inclusivity, inviting newcomers into the fold and fostering curiosity about an art form that previously may have seemed esoteric or reserved for the initiated. By breaking down barriers and providing entry points for exploration, tea leaf reading evolves into a rich communal experience that honors the traditions of the past while embracing the possibilities of the future.

In summary, digital communities and resources play a transformative role in the practice of tasseography, amplifying personal interpretations and fostering a sense of connectivity among practitioners. By sharing insights, engaging in discussions, and leveraging digital tools, individuals are not only deepening their understanding of tea leaf reading but also celebrating the collective wisdom woven into this art form. The evolving landscape of digital engagement paves the way for a renaissance in tea leaf reading, inviting practitioners to explore the layers of meaning hidden within the leaves while building vibrant connections with others who share their passion for this captivating craft.

11. Challenges and How to Overcome Them

11.1. Common Challenges Faced by Readers

In the enchanting world of tea leaf reading, practitioners often face a myriad of challenges as they navigate the intricate process of interpreting shapes and symbols. These challenges can arise from various aspects of the practice, including personal doubts, societal skepticism, and the complexities of understanding the tea leaves themselves. This chapter delves into the common challenges faced by readers and offers insights into how to overcome these obstacles, fostering a more enriching and rewarding experience in tea leaf readings.

One significant challenge encountered by readers, especially those new to tasseography, is the initial uncertainty regarding their ability to interpret the shapes formed by tea leaves. The process of deciphering these symbols can feel daunting; many practitioners grapple with self-doubt, fearing that they may misinterpret the signs or oversimplify the meanings derived from them. This ignited uncertainty often brings about a paralyzing fear of judgment—not only from themselves but also from others who may witness their readings.

To overcome this challenge, it is vital for aspiring tea leaf readers to cultivate self-compassion and trust in their intuition. Emphasizing the subjective nature of readings allows readers to acknowledge that interpretations may differ significantly among practitioners, reinforcing that there is no single "correct" way to analyze tea leaves. Engaging in regular practice enhances one's familiarity with the symbols and nurtures the intuitive skills that are integral to tea leaf reading. By journaling insights, using platforms like Emacs for documentation, and allowing oneself the freedom to explore interpretations, readers can gradually build confidence in their abilities while expanding their understanding of the symbols' meanings.

Another prevalent challenge is the skepticism surrounding the practice, both internally and externally. Many readers encounter disbelief from their social circles or face doubt within themselves regarding the validity of tea leaf readings as a form of divination. This skepticism can overshadow the practice, leading individuals to question their abilities and, ultimately, detracting from the reading experience.

To navigate this challenge, practitioners can adopt strategies that reaffirm their commitment to the art. Engaging in self-reflection allows individuals to align their readings with their own beliefs and experiences, helping to mitigate feelings of doubt. By documenting positive insights gained through readings or noting instances where tea leaf interpretations aligned with personal experiences, readers can create a reservoir of affirmations that counteract skepticism. Furthermore, discussing experiences with supportive communities—online or in-person—can provide encouragement and validation, reinforcing the essence of the practice.

Resilience within tea leaf reading is another critical aspect. Practitioners may face challenges in dealing with unclear or ambiguous readings. It is not uncommon to encounter situations where shapes formed by the leaves do not yield immediate insights, or where interpretations feel disconnected from one's current life circumstances. This lack of clarity can be both frustrating and disheartening, prompting readers to question the practice altogether.

To cultivate resilience, readers can approach these ambiguous moments with patience and curiosity. Instead of forcing rigid interpretations, they can regard unclear readings as opportunities to explore deeper layers of meaning or as moments signaling a need for self-reflection. Keeping an open-hearted approach allows individuals to sit with the uncertainty, embracing it as part of the reflective process. Documenting these experiences can also provide valuable context for future readings, highlighting patterns that may surface over time and enhancing one's understanding of the practice.

Finally, during challenging times, adaptability becomes crucial in maintaining a consistent tea leaf reading practice. Life events—such as personal loss, changes in circumstances, or heightened stress—can impact one's ability to engage fully with the ritual. These challenges can provoke feelings of disconnection from the practice, leading individuals to put their readings aside.

In overcoming this, readers can adjust their expectations and embrace flexibility in their ritual. Developing shorter, more focused reading sessions during challenging periods allows practitioners to maintain their connection to the practice without feeling overwhelmed. Rather than engaging in elaborate readings, simple reflections or mindful moments with tea can serve as a grounding practice, fostering an ongoing relationship with tasseography.

Reflecting on one's progress and growth acknowledges the evolution in interpretation skills, emotional resilience, and personal understanding. Practitioners can celebrate their journeys—recognizing the milestones achieved, the insights gained, and the many paths unveiled through the art of tasseography. Keeping an open dialogue with oneself encourages acknowledgment of both successes and challenges, reinforcing the rewarding aspects of the practice.

In conclusion, while common challenges abound in the realm of tea leaf reading, practitioners have the tools and strategies needed to overcome these obstacles. Embracing self-compassion, reinforcing belief in one's intuitive capabilities, fostering resilience, and adapting practices during difficult times empowers individuals to navigate the complexities of tasseography. Through patience and perseverance, readers can deepen their connection to both the art of tea leaf reading and the personal insights it offers, ensuring a fulfilling and transformative journey ahead.

11.2. Overcoming Skepticism and Doubt

In the practice of tea leaf reading, commonly referred to as tasseography, skepticism and doubt can act as formidable barriers to the fluidity and intuition vital for effective interpretation. Whether stemming from personal uncertainties, external criticisms, or societal perceptions, conquering these feelings is essential for practitioners eager to deepen their understanding and experience of this mystical art. This section explores actionable strategies that both novice and seasoned tea leaf readers can employ to overcome skepticism and doubt and foster a more confident engagement with their practice.

One of the primary sources of skepticism comes from internal doubt regarding one's ability to interpret the shapes and symbols formed by tea leaves. New practitioners may struggle with the fear of misinterpretation or not accurately connecting with the messages the leaves convey. To combat this feeling, it is crucial to cultivate self-compassion and understanding early on in one's journey. Recognizing that tasseography is as much an art as a science allows readers to embrace the fluidity of interpretation. Each shape and symbol drawn from the leaves invites personal engagement and is often subjective; embracing this subjectivity ensures that no one interpretation is inherently "right" or "wrong."

To address personal doubt, practitioners are encouraged to adopt a practice of recording their readings in a consistent manner. Using tools like Emacs allows for easy documentation and reflection, promoting the exploration of interpretations without the fear of judgment. Creating a dedicated organizational system for these entries can help establish a deeper connection with the practice. When readers can revisit previous insights and interpretations, they can track their growth, reinforce their understanding of recurring symbols, and develop confidence in their interpretative abilities. The act of documenting insights cultivates a sense of ownership and transparency in the journey, progressively easing the burden of skepticism.

Engaging with a supportive community also plays a significant role in overcoming skepticism and doubt. Finding groups or online forums dedicated to tea leaf reading can provide a space for reassurance, encouragement, and validation. Fellow practitioners can share their experiences, tips, and successes while collectively addressing common concerns. Group discussions often reveal that others grapple with similar doubts, thus allowing individuals to recognize that they are not alone in their feelings. The collaborative spirit nurtured within these communities enhances motivation and reaffirms that tea leaf reading is a shared journey of exploration rather than an isolated endeavor.

In addition to community support, fostering an environment of transparency allows practitioners to thrive. Encouraging open discussions about expectations around readings can further clarify misconceptions about the practice. As readers communicate their apprehensions and uncertainties with each other, they can collectively establish realistic standards for what tea leaf reading can offer. This dialogue reinforces the understanding that interpretations suggest possibilities rather than fixed outcomes, alleviating the pressure often associated with revealing the future.

As practitioners continue their journeys, adopting a mindset of curiosity can be profoundly beneficial. Rather than approaching readings with a focus on deciphering predetermined messages, embracing the exploration of the shapes formed by the leaves invites more authentic insights. Encouraging an inquisitive approach fosters openness and acceptance—qualities vital for successful readings. This perspective engages readers in a continual learning process, allowing them to appreciate the richness of interpretation that lies within differing shapes and symbols.

Moreover, individuals can tackle external skepticism head-on by emphasizing the personal significance derived from their readings. Practitioners should recognize that tea leaf reading hinges on the resonance that the interpretations have in their lives, regardless of the skepticism encountered from others. By focusing on their personal experiences, readers empower themselves to seek meaning without being swayed by doubt. The affirmation of personal relevance reinforces the notion that this practice is primarily for introspection and self-discovery, offering insights unique to each individual.

In conclusion, overcoming skepticism and doubt in tea leaf reading is an essential part of the journey toward deeper connections and insights. By cultivating self-compassion, documenting interpretations, engaging with supportive communities, fostering transparency, adopting curiosity, and recognizing the personal significance of read-ings, practitioners can dismantle barriers that hinder their practice. The exploration of tea leaves offers an invitation to embrace one's intuition and experiences, transforming skepticism into clarity—a process that ultimately enhances the magic of tasseography. As prac-titioners navigate their paths, they will find that understanding and acceptance pave the way for deeper self-discovery and connection with the ancient art of tea leaf reading.

11.3. Fostering Resilience in Your Practice

Fostering resilience in your practice of tea leaf reading is essential for deepening your connection to the art while enhancing your ability to interpret symbols and navigate life's complexities. Building resilience allows readers to face challenges, adapt to changes, and ultimately experience personal growth through their readings. As practitioners engage with the intricacies of tasseography, it is crucial to cultivate confidence, learn from experiences, and embrace the richness of the practice, regardless of external judgments or internal doubts.

Confidence is a cornerstone of resilience in tea leaf reading. The journey begins with acknowledging that no one is born with an innate ability to interpret tea leaves; rather, it is a skill developed through practice and patience. Each reading offers unique insights and expe-riences that contribute to your overall development as a reader. Embrace your journey by celebrating small victories and learning that mistakes are essential parts of growth. By adjusting your mindset to view challenges as opportunities for improvement, you strengthen your resilience and enhance your reading capabilities.

In overcoming self-doubt, it can be helpful to reflect on past read-ings and recognize how they have shaped your journey. Journaling your experiences and insights, perhaps through a tool like Emacs, encourages you to track your progress over time. Documenting your thoughts helps reinforce the connection between your interpretations and your own life experiences, allowing you to appreciate the trans-formative nature of the practice. As you observe your memories reflected in the shapes and symbols of tea leaves, you cultivate a deeper sense of trust in your intuition and the reading process.

Adapting your practice during challenging times is another crucial aspect of fostering resilience. Life is inherently unpredictable, and external factors can significantly impact your ability to engage in tea leaf readings regularly. During periods of stress, emotional turmoil, or personal upheaval, it may be beneficial to simplify your readings. Instead of conducting elaborate sessions, consider shorter, more focused readings that allow for reflection without feeling overwhelming. This approach encourages you to remain connected to the practice while also being gentle with yourself during difficult times.

Furthermore, engaging with a community of fellow practitioners amplifies resilience. Sharing experiences, insights, and challenges with others creates a supportive network where encouragement and understanding flourish. Participating in workshops, online forums, and discussions enables you to exchange knowledge about interpretation techniques while learning how other readers overcome their challenges. The collaborative spirit nurtured within these communities reinforces the importance of shared journeys and collective growth.

Another way to foster resilience is to embrace a mindset of curiosity and openness when reading the leaves. Rather than imposing rigid expectations, allow yourself the freedom to explore the realities of your interpretations. The beauty of tasseography lies in the personal nuances each reader brings to the shapes formed by the leaves; cultivating this exploration fosters adaptability and creative thinking in your practice. Approach each reading with a sense of wonder, ready to discover what insights might emerge, and recognize that every cup tells its own unique story.

Reflecting regularly on your progress and growth strengthens your resilience as a practitioner. Establishing a routine to review your readings—perhaps monthly—enables you to observe patterns, celebrate milestones, and recognize shifts in your interpretative process. This reflective practice fosters a sense of accomplishment, allowing you to appreciate the evolution of your understanding and approach to tasseography.

In conclusion, fostering resilience in your tea leaf reading practice is a dynamic and transformative journey that emphasizes building confidence, adapting through challenges, engaging with community, nurturing curiosity, and reflecting on progress. By looking inward and seeking connections with others, you deepen your engagement with the art of tasseography. Recognize that resilience is not merely about overcoming obstacles but about embracing the richness of each experience, empowering you to navigate life's complexities with grace, insight, and a renewed sense of purpose. As you embrace resilience, you allow tea leaf reading to become a powerful tool for personal growth, illuminating the path ahead with clarity and understanding.

11.4. Adapting During Challenging Times

In challenging times, as practitioners of tea leaf reading engage in tasseography, adapting their practices can lead to a deeper understanding of both the art and themselves. The act of reading tea leaves often brings unexpected revelations, but during periods of difficulty or uncertainty, it can also evoke feelings of doubt and hesitation. By harnessing the principles of resilience and flexibility, readers can transform their tea leaf readings into powerful tools for insight and growth, even in the most turbulent of times.

One cornerstone of adapting practices during challenging times involves embracing the inherent fluidity of both tea leaf readings and personal circumstances. Life is full of ebbs and flows, and recognizing that tea leaf reading is not solely about predicting a fixed future but rather exploring possibilities can invoke a sense of liberation. Practitioners should approach each reading as an opportunity to uncover insights related to the present moment, allowing themselves to be guided by the symbols that emerge from the leaves in response to their current emotional landscape.

When engaging in tea leaf readings, it can be beneficial to emphasize self-compassion. In times of heightened stress or anxiety, you may find that your readings feel less clear or that interpretations take on new meanings. It's crucial to remind yourself that this is part of the process. Having faith in your intuition and allowing space for uncertainty can pave the way for richer insights. You might contemplate shifting your reading focus, intentionally setting themes around personal resilience, adaptability, or emotional healing. These themes can ground your readings while illuminating pathways that resonate with your evolving experiences.

Engaging with your readings in real-time can be particularly helpful during periods of change. Rather than relying on strict interpretations, let the leaves themselves guide your reflections. When shapes form in the cup, take a moment to observe your immediate emotional reactions. Allow these feelings to influence your interpretations organically. Documenting your thoughts and insights as they arise—noticing how each shape resonates with your life events—can foster a strong connection between the intuitive signals from the tea leaves and the surrounding context of your life.

Creating a personalized ritual that aligns with your current needs can enhance this adaptive practice. For example, if you find yourself experiencing stress or difficulty, consider incorporating mindfulness techniques before your reading. Drawing on breathing exercises, visualization, or even grounding meditations can set a calming tone and prepare your mind to be truly present with the tea leaves. These practices allow you to transition gently into the reading, cultivating clarity and receptivity toward the messages that may unfold.

When navigating challenging times, it's also essential to maintain a social connection with fellow tea leaf readers. Utilizing digital platforms or online communities to share experiences can offer support, insight, and validation during difficult moments. Engaging in dialogues with those who understand the practice can remind you that you are not alone on this journey. Whether through group readings, interactive forums, or shared resources, being part of a community can create a comforting environment that encourages ongoing exploration and shared learning.

As readers adapt during challenging periods, they may discover new meanings in symbols that previously appeared straightforward. Keeping an open mind to re-evaluating interpretations enables practitioners to embrace the transformative nature of the symbols and the readings themselves. Tea leaf reading becomes a living practice that evolves as you confront and navigate life's complexities. By recognizing that every symbol carries multilayered meanings—especially in changing circumstances—practitioners deepen their reflective processes and adapt their interpretations in alignment with their personal journeys.

Finally, fostering an attitude of gratitude toward both the tea leaves and the insights they provide can revitalize your practice amid difficult times. Recognizing the wisdom in each reading, regardless of the clarity or depth of insights revealed, invites a perspective shift. Focusing on what you can learn from the process reinforces resilience and encourages you to embrace the multifaceted nature of tea leaf reading as a guiding companion on your path to self-discovery.

In summary, adapting practices during challenging times is vital for tea leaf readers striving for personal growth and insight. By cultivating self-compassion, engaging with readings in real-time, creating personalized rituals, maintaining community connections, and embracing the evolving nature of interpretation, practitioners can transform tea leaf readings into powerful supportive tools that guide them through life's complexities. Through this process, readers unveil a wealth of wisdom, enabling resilience that resonates deeply in their journeys of self-discovery.

11.5. Reflecting on Progress and Growth

In the practice of tea leaf reading, embracing the process of reflecting on progress and growth is not merely a retrospective exercise; it is a vital component of the journey that fosters deeper insights into both the practice and oneself. As practitioners engage with the mystical shapes formed by tea leaves, they inherently embark on a journey that intertwines intuition, emotional awareness, and personal discovery. This section delves into the significance of reflection in tea leaf reading and offers strategies for recognizing and harnessing the growth that unfolds through this ancient practice.

To commence this journey, practitioners must first recognize that every reading holds valuable lessons. The act of interpreting tea leaves creates an opportunity to explore not just the shapes within the cup, but also the emotional and situational contexts accompanying each reading. Practitioners are encouraged to cultivate a mindset that values progress in its myriad forms; whether that takes the shape of new insights, personal revelations, or an enhanced understanding of longstanding symbols observed in their readings.

Journaling becomes a critical tool in this process, providing an avenue through which readers can articulate their observations and reflections. By documenting interpretations in a structured manner, practitioners establish a record for future reference and analysis. Utilizing a robust platform like Emacs can enhance this documentation process, allowing readers to categorize insights, track patterns, and create reflective entries. This organized approach to journaling nurtures a deeper engagement with the symbols while encouraging readers to revisit past learnings and gauge their evolution over time.

As individuals reflect on their readings, maintaining a sense of curiosity is paramount. Tea leaf readings often yield rich interpretations, yet they may also provoke questions and uncertainty. Practitioners should remain open to this complexity, embracing moments of ambiguity as a natural part of the reading process. Reflecting on these uncertainties promotes growth as individuals examine how their feelings and experiences shape their interpretations. The practice of tea leaf reading becomes a lifelong exploration, where every session holds the potential for evolving understanding.

In addition to personal reflections, sharing insights with fellow practitioners can enhance growth. Engaging in discussions about readings, either in workshops or online communities, provides readers with diverse perspectives on their interpretations. This exchange fosters collective wisdom, enabling individuals to learn from one another while enhancing their own understanding of the symbols. The fluid nature of interpretations allows for collaborative observations that promote deeper contextual awareness and broaden the understanding of tea leaf reading as a whole.

Encouraging a practice of goal-setting can further align reflection with personal growth. After each reading, practitioners may wish to establish specific goals based on their insights. These goals can pertain to areas of life that require attention or exploration, allowing readers to actively engage with the revelations from their readings. By implementing actionable steps linked to the messages derived from the leaves, practitioners create pathways for personal transformation and reinforce the value of the practice as a guiding influence in their lives.

Moreover, revisiting past readings in light of new experiences can yield profound revelations. Practitioners might discover that the interpretations from earlier readings take on additional meaning as their life circumstances evolve. Engaging in a reflective cycle allows individuals to ponder how varying contexts can enrich their understanding of the symbols and shed light on ongoing challenges or aspirations. This cyclical awareness emphasizes that the lessons learned through tea leaf reading are not static but evolve alongside practitioner growth.

In summary, reflecting on progress and growth in the realm of tea leaf reading enhances the practitioner's journey toward self-discovery and insight. Through systematic journaling, sharing experiences with a community, embracing curiosity, setting goals, and revisiting past readings, individuals can deepen their connection to the practice. Ultimately, this reflection cultivates a dynamic relationship with both the tea leaves and the inner self, inviting a richer understanding of the symbols that guide the path ahead. As practitioners navigate the pages of their tea leaf explorations, they unveil not just the secrets held within the cups but also the profound journey that unfolds through every reading experience.

12. Symbol Interpretations: A Comprehensive Guide

12.1. Understanding Basic Symbols

Understanding the essential nature of symbols is pivotal in tea leaf reading, or tasseography, as it forms the cornerstone of interpretation and insight. The delicate shapes created by tea leaves, left behind in a cup after the beverage has been enjoyed, act as a powerful medium through which practitioners can glean meaningful insight into their lives, potential challenges, and future opportunities. This exploration of symbols lays the groundwork for comprehending the narratives hidden within the leaves, bridging the ancient practice of tasseography with personal growth and reflection.

To begin with, symbols in tea leaf reading can take on many forms, often reflecting the querent's emotional landscape, current life circumstances, or pressing questions. Understanding basic symbols commonly encountered in readings provides a robust framework that readers can reference as they navigate the intricacies of interpretation. With each shape, readers can unlock a language that speaks to intuitive insights, revealing connections between the reader, the leaves, and their broader life narratives.

Among the most recognizable symbols is the heart, which universally signifies love and relationships. In readings, it may represent a romantic connection or familial bonds, inviting practitioners to explore emotional insights surrounding their relationships. Conversely, the key symbolizes new beginnings and opportunities, urging readers to embrace change and be open to the potential unfolding of new paths in their lives. The star, often associated with hope and guidance, suggests that the querent should remain optimistic about their journey ahead, capturing the essence of aspiration.

Shapes resembling natural elements also carry substantial meanings. Circles often indicate wholeness or completion, pointing out a cycle that is culminating in the querent's life. Squares, on the other hand, can embody stability and security, highlighting the need for grounding amidst life's challenges. Each of these symbols encapsulates specific messages that readers can access, enriching the tapestry of interpretations as they relate to personal experiences.

Moreover, animal-themed symbols provide unique perspectives in readings. For example, a bird typically represents freedom and new perspectives, suggesting that the querent may be on the verge of receiving new information or communicating important feelings. A snake can indicate transformation, shedding of the old, and emergence into a new self. Recognizing the context of these animal symbols can deepen the insights drawn from the reading.

As tea leaf readers hone their skills, they may encounter uncommon symbols that deserve exploration. These might include abstract shapes or unique configurations that can emerge unexpectedly. Such symbols often invite a deeper level of interpretation, where practitioners rely on their intuition to uncover personal meanings. This adaptability in understanding reinforces the idea that while traditional interpretations provide essential guidance, each reading comprises an individual journey—where personal narratives can shift and evolve.

To enhance the reading experience, practitioners are encouraged to document their symbol interpretations in a thoughtful manner. Utilizing tools like Emacs can help manage this data effectively, allowing readers to create a personal lexicon that outlines each symbol's meanings, emotional resonance, and connections to past readings. This ongoing practice cultivates a rich resource that complements the art of tasseography, bolstering confidence and clarity as readers engage with their craft.

Ultimately, interpreting symbols in tea leaf reading is both an art and a science—a delicate blend of structured meanings with intuitive personal insights. By recognizing and analyzing the myriad symbols that emerge from tea leaves, practitioners can embark on a journey of self-discovery and depth, unlocking the narratives embedded in their cups. The beauty of tasseography lies in its ability to connect practitioners with the whispers of their inner selves, guiding them toward a deeper understanding of their current experiences and future potential. Embracing the language of symbolism ultimately transforms tea leaf readings into powerful tools for reflection, growth, and empowerment, inviting individuals to explore the stories crafted within each unique reading.

12.2. Advanced Symbol Interpretations

In the realm of tea leaf reading, understanding advanced symbol interpretations opens a doorway to a richer engagement with the intricate shapes formed by leaves left behind in a cup. As practitioners delve deeper into this mystical art, they encounter symbols that go beyond basic meanings, evolving into a complex language that speaks to personal, emotional, and spiritual insights. This journey requires an exploration of nuanced symbol interpretations, consideration of less common symbols, and the application of broader themes, ultimately enriching one's practice and understanding of tasseography.

Advanced symbol interpretation involves recognizing that symbols may shift and adapt based on context. Each symbol formed by tea leaves embodies layers of meaning that can respond to an individual's emotional state and life circumstances. A crescent moon might represent intuition and femininity, but in a context where a reader grapples with uncertainty, it could also suggest feelings of vulnerability or the need for self-reflection. By honing the skill of contextual analysis, practitioners can derive deeper insights reflective of their unique life experiences.

As readers cultivate their understanding of advanced symbols, they must also consider the subtleties of shape and arrangement. The proximity of symbols to one another, their size, and their orientation can further inform their meaning. For example, two symbols closely aligned might indicate interconnected themes—such as love and trust —whereas a solitary symbol could evoke isolation or introspection. By examining the overall composition of the shapes, practitioners develop a more nuanced interpretation that resonates within the context of the querent's life situation.

Throughout this journey, the exploration of uncommon symbols presents an opportunity to engage with tea leaf reading from fresh perspectives. While familiar shapes such as hearts, stars, and keys are commonplace, readings may occasionally reveal unique symbols that prompt deeper inquiry. Uncommon symbols such as feathers—often associated with communication and freedom—can provide rich narratives based on the practitioner's understanding of their meanings. Similarly, symbols like spirals or infinity signs may evoke themes of growth, transformation, or continuity.

Documenting encounters with uncommon symbols can expand the reader's personal lexicon, nurturing a deeper understanding of their significance over time. Using platforms like Emacs to create a comprehensive symbol dictionary can be particularly beneficial. By curating interpretations based on emotional resonance and past readings, readers can reference a reservoir of collective wisdom that informs their practices, enhancing their intution and insight.

In tandem with individual interpretations, the integration of digital resources serves to bridge the gap between advanced interpretations and broader symbolic lexicons. Reading literature, visiting dedicated websites, and engaging in online communities devoted to tasseography can facilitate collaborative discussions on symbols, providing invaluable insights and interpretations that enhance the reader's own skills. Engaging in thoughtful exchanges cultivates an appreciation for the diversity of perspectives while appreciating the beauty of the art itself.

Additionally, employing visual aids during readings can significantly reinforce interpretations. Observing patterns closely and sketching shapes can facilitate engagement with the symbols on a deeper level. Practitioners can employ Emacs to create visual representations and analyses, promoting an enriching understanding of how specific symbols manifest through various contexts.

Ultimately, as practitioners delve into advanced symbol interpretations, they unlock a wealth of insight that enriches their practice of tasseography. By embracing context, exploring less common symbols, and fostering an inquisitive approach, tea leaf readings transform from simple divinations into profound journeys of self-discovery and connection. This level of engagement invites readers to become more attuned not only to the whispers of the tea leaves but also to the narratives that unfold within their own lives, creating a tapestry of meaning that resonates deeply with the essence of the practice.

12.3. Uncommon Symbols and Their Mysteries

Uncommon symbols hold a special place in the art of tea leaf reading, or tasseography, as they invite deeper exploration and stimulate the imagination. While the more commonly recognized symbols—like hearts, stars, and keys—serve as foundational elements for practitioners, unusual shapes can often reveal profound insights and narratives that traditional symbols may not encompass. This section delves into the allure of these uncommon symbols, their potential meanings, and the mysteries they may convey during a reading.

Uncommon symbols can emerge from the unpredictable nature of tea leaves settling in the cup, often manifesting as obscure shapes, abstract formations, or blends of familiar symbols that take on new meanings. Such symbols challenge practitioners to explore their intuitive faculties deeply, offering a rich landscape for interpretation that transcends standard readings. For example, a shape resembling a labyrinth or spiral might suggest a winding journey of self-discovery, urging the querent to embrace their personal path despite the complexities encountered.

As readers encounter these unique shapes, it is vital to approach the interpretation process with an open mind and a sense of curiosity. One might wonder whether a symbol's rarity reflects its significance —what truths lie beneath the surface of these shapes? Practitioners are encouraged to observe their emotional reactions and intuitive impressions when seeing uncommon symbols, as these responses often signal a deeper connection to the reading and the querent's life.

Additionally, it may be beneficial to create a dedicated log for uncommon symbols observed during readings. Using a tool such as Emacs, practitioners can catalog these rare shapes, documenting personal interpretations and the feelings evoked during each encounter. This ongoing collection becomes a valuable resource, enabling readers to reflect on their encounters with uncommon symbols and discern patterns in their meanings over time. By systematically analyzing how particular shapes resonate across readings, practitioners deepen their understanding of symbolism while honing their intuitive skills.

The meaning ascribed to these uncommon symbols can also draw from broader cultural or historical contexts. Practitioners may find inspiration in mythology, art, or even literature, incorporating these references when interpreting shapes as they connect the symbol with the querent's personal narrative. For instance, a butterfly might represent transformation due to its associations with metamorphosis across cultures. This expansive approach allows readers to breathe life into their interpretations, enriching the meanings and encouraging a deeper connection to the practice.

Furthermore, engaging with community forums and online resources can shed light on less common symbols encountered in readings. Fellow practitioners may share their experiences, providing insights that reveal alternative interpretations or collective cultural knowledge surrounding specific shapes. By listening to diverse perspectives and integrating shared narratives into their personal practice, readers can cultivate a broader and more nuanced understanding of uncommon symbols.

Ultimately, the exploration of uncommon symbols in tea leaf reading serves as an invitation to discover the deeper mysteries woven into the act of tasseography. By engaging with these unique shapes and remaining open to the varied interpretations they inspire, practitioners enrich their connection to the practice and deepen their intuition. Through this journey, the leaves reveal their secrets and guide practitioners toward greater self-discovery, creativity, and meaningful insights—a continuous dance of understanding that harmonizes the familiar with the elusive.

As one embraces the mysteries presented by uncommon symbols, the art of tea leaf reading transforms into an ever-evolving journey, inviting practitioners to be both explorers and interpreters in their quest for insight and personal growth.

To further enhance your knowledge of uncommon symbols and their meanings, practitioners may consider establishing a comprehensive symbol dictionary. This resource could serve as a guide, enriching their understanding of both traditional and unconventional symbols encountered in tea leaf readings. Developing this dictionary, perhaps using an Emacs framework, allows readers to reference symbols quickly, contributing greatly to their journey in tasseography.

This symbol dictionary could include not only visual representations of each shape but also their interpretations, cultural significance, and personal anecdotes that readers have gathered over time, forming a multi-dimensional resource that evolves with their practice. As a living document, it captures the richness of the tea leaf reading journey in its entirety. Understanding uncommon symbols in tea leaf readings ultimately invites practitioners to engage deeply with their intuition and personal experiences, enhancing the beauty and significance of this ancient practice.

12.4. Symbol Dictionaries and Resources

In the realm of tea leaf reading, symbol dictionaries and resources serve as invaluable tools that enrich the practitioner's understanding of the intricate language of tea leaves. Tasseography, with its roots in ancient traditions, invites readers to explore the depths of symbolism embedded in the patterns formed by leaves settled in a cup. As readers embark on this interpretative journey, having access to curated symbol dictionaries and resources can enhance their practice, providing clarity and depth to the readings that unfold before them.

A symbol dictionary specific to tea leaf reading captures a rich lexicon of shapes and interpretations, providing a comprehensive reference point for practitioners to consult during their readings. Such resources typically categorize symbols based on common shapes—the heart, the star, the crescent moon—and offer context-specific meanings tied to cultural influences and traditional lore. By documenting the symbols encountered over countless readings, each practitioner contributes to the collective wisdom of the community, creating a living repository of insights that continues to evolve.

These dictionaries can be formatted for easy navigation and accessibility, utilizing tools like Emacs to create an organized database that can be quickly referenced. Practitioners can categorize symbols by their visual characteristics, emotional resonance, or the specific life themes they evoke. This level of organization empowers readers to connect their personal experiences with broader symbolic meanings, enriching their interpretations as they adapt their understandings according to their unique readings.

In addition to traditional symbols, advanced dictionaries can also include uncommon symbols that emerge in specific readings. These shapes may carry layers of meaning that require exploration, prompting readers to document and unpack the significance of the journeys these unusual symbols take them on. By adding personal reflections alongside the symbols recorded, practitioners create a deeper pool of knowledge that they can revisit over time—catalyzing growth in their intuitive abilities and enhancing their connection to the tea leaf reading practice.

Resources that accompany symbol dictionaries can extend beyond simple lists and definitions. Practical guides that offer insight into the historical significance of particular symbols, cultural associations, or variations found across different regions round out the understanding of tasseography. Such resources encourage readers to view symbols through a broader lens, fostering an appreciation for the layers of interpretation that derive from diverse cultural contexts and individual experiences.

Moreover, collaborative platforms—be they forums, social media groups, or dedicated websites—act as fertile grounds for sharing knowledge about symbols and their meanings. Readers can connect and exchange insights, allowing for mutual exploration of shapes that have surprised or intrigued them during their own tea leaves readings. This collaborative knowledge-sharing not only deepens the understanding of symbols but also helps create a supportive community of practitioners eager to enhance their craft together.

Workshops and community gatherings also play a pivotal role in symbol exploration. During these sessions, participants can engage in hands-on practice, examining symbols collectively and sharing interpretations based on their individual readings. This interactive setting fosters a sense of belonging while encouraging the discovery of new perspectives and contexts for understanding the symbols present in each reading.

In essence, the existence of symbol dictionaries and resources within the practice of tea leaf reading serves to elevate the experience and deepen the connections practitioners hold with their art. Beloved by seasoned readers and newcomers alike, these resources empower practitioners to explore, learn, and grow as they navigate the mystical language of tea leaves. By embracing the insights derived from a vast array of symbols, readers can illuminate their paths toward self-discovery, reflection, and personal transformation, enriching both their individual journeys and the collective experience of the tea leaf reading community.

12.5. Visual Aids in Symbol Recognition

In tea leaf reading, the practice of interpreting symbols often benefits greatly from the use of visual aids, which can enhance understanding and recognition of the various shapes that tea leaves create. Visual aids can range from sketches and charts to digital representations, and they play an important role in making the meanings more accessible and relatable for readers. By employing visual tools, practitioners not only deepen their connection with the symbols but also foster a more intuitive approach that complements their analytical skills.

One practical application of visual aids is hosting workshops or group readings where participants are encouraged to sketch the shapes they observe in their cups of tea. As each participant draws their interpretation, a lively discussion can ensue, with individuals sharing their insights and the meanings they ascribe to the symbols. This collaborative process not only reinforces learning but also builds camaraderie within the group, allowing participants to form a robust community foundation where knowledge and creativity flow freely.

Additionally, practitioners can utilize digital tools to create a visual catalog of common and uncommon symbols found in tea leaf readings. This can be accomplished using platforms like Emacs, which can organize data, categorize symbols, and create an easy reference guide. By incorporating images or sketches of the various shapes along with their meanings, practitioners cultivate a comprehensive resource that encourages intuitive engagement. This catalog can serve as a visual language that resonates with readers, enhancing their interpretative skills over time.

Advanced Emacs users can take this a step further by creating interactive tools that allow readers to link specific symbols to personalized references, emotional responses, and life experiences. This integration fosters a deeper connection with the shapes formed by the leaves, transforming the ritual into a comprehensive exploration of both intuitive and practical insights. By embedding personal narratives alongside symbols, practitioners can develop richer interpretations that reflect their journeys of self-discovery.

Moreover, visual aids serve to demystify the readings, making the insights more approachable and relatable. As practitioners become more comfortable with identifying shapes and connecting them to emotions or life circumstances, they can create their own visual language tailored to their unique experiences. This process reinforces the idea that reading tea leaves transcends mere interpretation; it is a practice deeply entwined with individual stories and contexts.

In conclusion, the incorporation of visual aids in tea leaf reading significantly enhances the interpretative experience for practitioners. Through sketches, digital catalogs, collaborative discussions, and personal connections, readers can navigate the intricate language of tea leaves with greater ease and confidence. As they delve deeper into the meanings encompassed within each shape, visual tools illuminate their practice, transforming the art of tasseography into a dynamic journey of insight, creativity, and community. This enriching engagement emphasizes that, ultimately, the leaves reveal their secrets not only through their shapes but also through the connections readers forge in the process.

13. Balancing Ancient Practices and Modern Approaches

13.1. Respecting Tradition in Modern Contexts

In the ever-evolving landscape of tea leaf reading, respecting tradition while adapting to modern contexts forms a delicate balance that practitioners must navigate. Tasseography, with its rich history and deep cultural roots, offers profound insights and opportunities for self-discovery that should be honored even as contemporary interpretations encourage innovation. As readers delve into the art of interpreting tea leaves through the lens of modernity, they must consider how to honor the practice's heritage while integrating new tools and methods that broaden its appeal and accessibility.

First, acknowledging the historical significance and cultural contexts of tea leaf reading helps ground the practice in its authenticity. Practitioners should educate themselves about the origins of tasseography, tracing its lineage back to various cultures and the meanings ascribed to specific symbols and shapes. Elements of various traditions, including Chinese, Greek, and Victorian influences, shape how tea leaves are interpreted and understood today. By respecting these legacies, practitioners create a richer context for their readings, allowing for a deeper engagement with the symbols drawn from tea.

In adapting to modern contexts, practitioners can blend this respect for tradition with contemporary advancements. The advent of technology provides tools that can enhance the experience of tea leaf reading, capturing and organizing insights in ways that traditional methods may not easily accommodate. Platforms like Emacs offer flexibility in documenting readings, categorizing insights, and facilitating meaningful analysis over time. By creating a digital space anchored in the practice's historical significance, contemporary readers can share their experiences while paying homage to the past.

The challenge lies in finding harmony between these old and new approaches. This harmony is best achieved by integrating traditional techniques—like mindful observation and personal reflection—with modern practices. For example, while interpreting tea leaves today, practitioners can still engage in the ceremonial aspects of brewing and enjoying tea, thereby honoring the legacy of the ritual. Simultaneously, they might introduce elements such as collaborative online workshops, forum discussions, or the use of digital journals to evolve the practice into something accessible and relevant to contemporary practitioners.

Cultural sensitivity plays a crucial role in this fusion of tradition and modernity. As tea leaf reading continues to gain popularity worldwide, practitioners should remain aware of the diverse cultural backgrounds that inform the practice. This acknowledgment includes recognizing and respecting the nuances inherent in interpretations derived from various regions and traditions. It is essential to approach the symbols with an open heart and an understanding that contextual meanings may vary across cultures. Engaging in conversations that explore these cultural dimensions fosters inclusivity and enriches the tapestry of tea leaf reading.

As innovations in modern tasseography emerge, practitioners should remain open to exploring new methodologies that may elevate their practice. Whether through technological integrations, enhanced documentation strategies, or new interpretive frameworks, these innovations can breathe fresh life into the art of tea leaf reading, allowing it to flourish while respecting its roots. For example, the potential for artificial intelligence to analyze reading patterns and suggest interpretations based on historical data can enhance the traditional art form—offering practitioners a balanced view that bridges the mystical and the analytical.

Encouraging an open-minded approach allows practitioners to nurture creativity and adaptability within their practice. By embracing the idea that tea leaf reading can evolve while maintaining its core essence, readers create a dynamic landscape for self-exploration and insight. This adaptability invites practitioners to explore innovative techniques, integrate new perspectives, and share their journeys with others.

In conclusion, as practitioners of tasseography navigate the complexities of respecting tradition in modern contexts, they unlock the potential for tea leaf reading to serve as an enduring bridge between the past and the present. By honoring the legacies, embracing innovative tools, fostering cultural sensitivity, and remaining open to evolving practices, readers can forge a path that is both respectful of the roots of tea leaf reading and vibrant with the possibilities of the future. In this intersection of ancient wisdom and contemporary insights, the journey of tea leaf reading invites self-discovery, community connection, and appreciation for the enduring art waiting to be unveiled in every cup.

13.2. Finding Harmony Between Old and New

Finding harmony between the old and the new in tea leaf reading, or tasseography, represents a captivating blend of tradition and innovation, threading together the rich heritage of this ancient practice with the opportunities offered by modern technology. As practitioners engage with the mystical world of tea leaves, it becomes essential to explore how traditional practices can thrive alongside contemporary advancements, enriching the insights yielded from each reading and enhancing connection between readers and their intuitive selves.

At the heart of this exploration is the acknowledgment of the centuries-old customs that have shaped tea leaf reading over time. From its origins in ancient cultures, where tea was revered not just as a beverage but as a means of connection to the universe, to its evolution into a practice that resonates profoundly in today's world, the foundations of tasseography invite respect and appreciation. Practitioners often engage with symbols that encompass layers of historical significance, drawing on both cultural narratives and personal experiences that color their interpretations of the shapes formed by tea leaves.

However, as tea leaf reading enters the digital age, practitioners are presented with the unique opportunity to leverage technological advancements that enhance their practice. Emacs, for instance, stands out as a versatile tool that can aid in documenting readings, organizing interpretations, and fostering a community of likeminded practitioners. The adaptability of this software allows for the establishment of structured templates, prompting readers to capture not only the shapes revealed in their cups but also the emotions and thoughts that accompany their interpretations. By using technology to streamline processes, the essence of the practice is preserved while simultaneously inviting new dimensions of engagement.

Balancing the respect for traditional practices with modern approaches necessitates an open dialogue among practitioners. Through community discussions—whether in person or in digital forums—individuals can share ideas about how to honor the roots of tea leaf reading while embracing innovation. These exchanges promote a collective exploration of the evolving role of technology and how it can enhance emotional intelligence and intuition in readings. By weaving together the wisdom of experienced readers with the fresh perspectives of newcomers, the practice flourishes, inviting diverse interpretations and enriching the collective understanding of symbols.

Moreover, the marriage of tradition and innovation manifests in the diversification of symbolism within tea leaf reading. As practitioners encounter uncommon shapes, they are encouraged to transcend rigid interpretations and engage in a more fluid process that synthesizes both established meanings and personal associations. This adaptability allows readers to view the leaves as reflective mirrors of their lives, fostering growth and insight through nuanced interactions that blend the old with the new.

Importantly, practitioners can embrace creative expression alongside structured interpretations. As technology broadens access to tea leaf reading resources, individuals are empowered to explore their unique artistry within the practice. They may choose to sketch the shapes they observe or document readings with visual flair, combining tradition with personal expression. Initiating workshops where participants illustrate their interpretations or share experiences enriches collaboration and fosters a sense of community.

Ultimately, the essence of finding harmony between the old and the new lies in allowing tea leaf reading to evolve while remaining anchored in authenticity. Practitioners can embrace the advancements in technology, engage in collaborative learning, and remain open to the emerging dimensions that this captivating art form can embody. In doing so, they position themselves as stewards of both tradition and progress, gifting future generations a resilient practice that honors cultural heritage while embracing the transformative power of innovation.

As tea leaf readers embark on this journey, they are invited to explore the myriad possibilities that arise from merging the past with the present. Navigating this intersection enriches personal intuition and fosters connections to the broader tapestry of human experience, illuminating the wisdom found within each reading. The harmonious blend of old and new reflects the ongoing evolution of tasseography, transforming it into an inviting practice that promises insight, growth, and an enduring legacy.

13.3. Cultural Sensitivity in Modern Divination

Cultural sensitivity in modern divination is crucial, particularly in the context of tea leaf reading, or tasseography. As practitioners navigate this ancient practice interwoven with contemporary influences, it is essential to recognize and respect the diverse cultural backgrounds and traditions that inform the interpretations of tea leaves. This subchapter delves into the importance of understanding cultural nuances, honoring traditions, and fostering an inclusive atmosphere within the tea leaf reading community.

Tea leaf reading has origins across various cultures, notably in the customs surrounding tea consumption in countries such as China, India, and Turkey. Each of these cultures carries unique beliefs, interpretations, and rituals associated with the practice. To honor these traditions is to admit the richness they bring to contemporary readings. It is, therefore, the responsibility of modern practitioners to educate themselves about the history of tasseography and the cultural significance of the symbols they encounter. This foundational awareness allows readers to approach their practice with respect and appreciation for the legacies that precede them.

Furthermore, when interpreting the shapes formed by tea leaves, readers should be mindful of how cultural interpretations influence their readings. The symbolism of certain shapes may vary widely among cultures; for instance, a crescent may symbolize intuition and potential in one context while embodying loss or longing in another. Practitioners must remain open to these differences, avoiding the temptation to impose a single narrative or interpretation based solely on their personal understanding. Embracing a diverse range of insights fosters an enriching practice, rewarding readers with expansive perspectives that enhance their interpretations and personal growth.

Encouraging inclusivity within the tea leaf reading community is another facet of cultural sensitivity. By creating welcoming spaces for practitioners from diverse backgrounds, readers can cultivate a collaborative environment where different interpretations can flourish. Open dialogues where individuals share their unique perspectives on symbols, grounded in their cultural histories, can deepen the understanding of tasseography as a living, breathing art form. These interactions emphasize the idea that every practitioner contributes valuable insights that enrich the collective knowledge surrounding tea leaf reading, acknowledging that each interpretation is colored by personal and cultural lenses.

Moreover, digital platforms provide a unique opportunity to foster cultural sensitivity in modern tea leaf reading practices. Online forums, social media groups, and virtual workshops can connect practitioners globally, allowing for substantial cultural exchanges. These platforms empower individuals to share their experiences, interpretations, and creative insights, contributing to a rich narrative that transcends boundaries. By collaborating and learning from one another, practitioners can refine their skills while elevating their sensitivity to cultural contexts.

Engaging with literature centered around tea leaf reading, including historical texts, cultural research, or contributions from diverse practitioners, further informs cultural sensitivity. Readers can explore how tea leaf reading has evolved over time, gaining insights into the myriad interpretations that exist within the practice. By studying the origins of tea drinking and its conciliatory role throughout history, practitioners can better appreciate the symbolism that arises within their readings and create a harmonious connection with their heritage.

Additionally, a commitment to ongoing learning encourages practitioners to remain aware of cultural nuances as they engage in tea leaf readings. This involves recognizing the context in which symbols are interpreted, allowing practitioners to navigate sensitive topics with care. Acknowledging that personal experiences can shape emotional responses to readings helps practitioners approach the practice authentically, showing respect for the intricate tapestry of lives that inform each cup of tea.

In conclusion, cultural sensitivity in modern divination, particularly within the tea leaf reading community, is essential for fostering inclusive and respectful practices. By acknowledging the historical and cultural significance of symbols, embracing diverse perspectives, and promoting open dialogue, practitioners enhance their engagements with tasseography. As readers navigate the beautiful intersection of tradition and contemporary insights, they create a deeper connection with the practice, enriching their personal journeys while honoring the vast tapestry of cultures that have contributed to the art of tea leaf reading. This cultural awareness not only broadens personal interpretations but also nurtures a sense of community and connection amongst practitioners, encouraging empathy and understanding as they explore the mysteries hidden within their cups.

13.4. Innovations in Modern Tasseography

In the ever-evolving landscape of tea leaf reading, or tasseography, modern innovations have breathed new life into this ancient practice, transforming how practitioners engage with the art of interpretation.

The just undercurrent of technology, creativity, and a growing interest in personal development signals exciting changes ahead for both novice and experienced readers alike. This section delves into the various advancements influencing the field, presenting opportunities for a richer understanding of the symbols and their meanings while maintaining the essence of tradition that defines tea leaf reading.

At the core of these innovations lies the integration of technological tools that enhance the reading experience. For instance, software like Emacs allows practitioners to document their readings systematically, capturing insights and interpretations in a structured format. The versatility of Emacs enables users to organize their notes, creating a personal lexicon of symbols and their meanings. As readers engage in ongoing documentation, they develop a comprehensive repository of knowledge that reflects their growth and evolving understanding of the practice.

Moreover, these technological advancements have led to what some may refer to as the democratization of tea leaf reading. Practitioners now have access to online forums, social media groups, and dedicated websites that connect tea leaf readers from across the globe. These digital spaces foster community interaction, allowing individuals to share readings, ask questions, and discuss interpretations freely. The immediate exchange of knowledge serves to enrich the practitioner's experience, providing diverse perspectives that enhance the understanding of traditional symbols while inviting innovative interpretations.

In addition to technology-driven insights, there is also a discernible shift in the approach to interpreting symbols. Practitioners increasingly recognize that meanings are not static; they evolve based on personal experiences, societal changes, and cultural influences. This dynamic perspective invites practitioners to embrace a broader understanding of tea leaf interpretations, encouraging flexibility in how symbols are perceived and understood. As practitioners explore these new dimensions, they discover that every shape left by the tea leaves offers an opportunity for deeper introspection and inquiry—a call for more personalized connections to the symbols formed by the leaves.

Furthermore, workshops and group readings are experiencing a renaissance as practitioners gather to share their insights in collaborative settings. These communal gatherings provide a unique opportunity for readers to engage with one another, exchanging interpretations and building a collective knowledge base. As participants share their experiences, they contribute to a communal narrative that enhances the overall practice, allowing for a richer exploration of the symbols encountered in tea readings. This emphasis on collaboration strengthens the foundations of the tea leaf reading community, fostering connection and support among practitioners.

Creativity plays a substantial role in the current innovations within tea leaf reading as well. Practitioners are increasingly encouraged to infuse artistic expression into their readings, whether through sketching, journaling, or incorporating visual elements that resonate with them. This personalized approach not only deepens the connection to the tea leaves but also invites readers to explore their individual narratives, enhancing emotional engagement and intuition during readings.

As the world continues to change, so too will the art of tea leaf reading. Embracing a mindset that welcomes adaptive practices while remaining respectful of tradition fosters a mindful exploration of both the subtleties of the symbols and the broader narratives they convey. The opportunity to redefine how tasseography is practiced in modern contexts encourages both experienced readers and newcomers to embark on a journey marked by curiosity, creativity, and personal growth.

Overall, the future of tea leaf reading heralds an exciting time of synthesis between ancient practices and modern innovations. As practitioners navigate this evolving landscape, they continue to uncover the potential hidden within each cup, learning that tea leaves whisper not only their secrets but also the stories of all who engage with their timeless art. The fusion of technology, community, and creativity emphasizes the enduring significance of tasseography, inviting every reader to explore their unique path in the captivating world of tea leaf readings.

13.5. Remaining Open to Evolving Practices

Remaining open to evolving practices within the realm of tea leaf reading—tasseography—encourages a dynamic exploration of one of humanity's most captivating arts. In this rapidly changing world, where traditional practices often intersect with modern philosophies and technologies, maintaining an adaptable mindset becomes crucial for both experienced readers and newcomers alike. Embracing this fluidity not only enhances personal interpretations but also enriches the communal landscape of tea leaf reading, inviting practitioners to weave their unique narratives into the ancient fabric of this mystical practice.

In recognizing the evolving nature of tasseography, practitioners are encouraged to reflect on how their journey influences their understanding of the tea leaves and the symbols they uncover. Each reading serves as a snapshot of the present, shaped by personal experiences, emotions, and life circumstances. As readers navigate through the shifting sands of their lives, they may find that their interpretations transform alongside their evolving perspectives. The willingness to adapt and embrace new insights enables individuals to deepen their connection with the symbols found in tea leaves, illuminating paths previously overlooked.

Readers should also consider the role of technology in refining their perspectives on tea leaf reading. Digital tools, such as Emacs, open new avenues for documenting interpretations, analyzing readings, and engaging with fellow practitioners. Utilizing these resources fosters a sense of community and collaboration, where practitioners can explore diverse interpretations and share their insights freely. As practitioners gather insights through modern avenues, they remain firmly rooted in the rich history of tasseography, creating a tapestry that combines tradition with innovative thought.

Moreover, fostering an openness to explore diverse methods of interpretation invites creativity and personal expression into the practice. Tea leaf readings can be enhanced by integrating art, journaling, or even storytelling, allowing practitioners to infuse their unique voices into the ritual. This approach transforms tea leaf reading from a static interpretation into a vibrant, ongoing dialogue with the self and the universe, wherein symbols evolve into narratives rich with meaning and insight.

This journey of openness extends beyond individual practice; it encompasses a collective embrace of diversity within the tea leaf reading community. Practitioners come from diverse cultural and experiential backgrounds, bringing varied interpretations and understandings to the art. By fostering inclusive dialogue, readers cultivate a space where all perspectives are honored and explored. This integration of community wisdom enriches the experience of tasseography, expanding the depth and breadth of readings that emerge from even a single teacup.

As practitioners remain open to evolving practices, they acknowledge that tea leaf reading is not a destination, but rather a continuous journey of exploration. Engaging with this art empowers readers to discover new dimensions of meaning while providing the grace to adapt to life's changes. Every symbol encountered in tea leaves offers an invitation—to embrace the mysteries of life, to learn and grow, and to connect deeply with oneself and others.

Embracing change is a testament to the living nature of tea leaf reading, and as each practitioner walks this path, they contribute to the collective heritage of this ancient practice. By cultivating a mindset rooted in curiosity, collaboration, and creativity, readers unlock the potential of each reading—transforming the ephemeral shapes formed by tea leaves into lasting connections to their own lives.

In conclusion, remaining open to evolving practices fosters a vibrant exploration of tasseography, paving the way for personal transformations and communal growth in the art of tea leaf reading. As each practitioner embraces the changes that unfold, they become not just interpreters of symbols but also participants in a larger narrative —a continuing story interwoven through generations, cultures, and experiences. In this journey, may practitioners discover not only the wisdom contained in their tea leaves but also the profound capacity for growth, understanding, and connection inherent in the practice itself.

14. Developing Intuition and Insight with Emacs

14.1. Harnessing Intuition in Readings

Harnessing intuition in tea leaf readings is an essential aspect of the practice that allows practitioners to access deeper insights, connect with their emotions, and uncover the meanings behind the symbols formed by the tea leaves in the cup. The art of tea leaf reading, or tasseography, requires not just analytical thinking but also a willingness to trust one's intuition and develop a connection with the leaves through observation and reflection. This section explores various strategies and approaches to help practitioners harness their intuition, enriching their tea leaf reading experience and deepening their understanding of the symbols present in their readings.

To begin, developing trust in one's intuition is key to effective tea leaf reading. This trust can be cultivated through intentional practice and a nurturing mindset. Establishing a regular tea leaf reading practice encourages familiarity with the shapes and symbols formed by the leaves, enhancing one's ability to discern and interpret their meanings. Whether you're reading alone or in a group setting, take note of your emotional responses, thoughts, and reflections during the reading process. Create a space for these insights to unfold organically, allowing intuition to guide you as you interpret the shapes left in the cup.

Mindfulness plays a critical role in this journey of harnessing intuition. Practitioners should approach each tea leaf reading with a sense of presence, consciously setting aside distractions and centering their thoughts. By engaging in mindfulness exercises before reading —such as deep breathing, meditation, or focusing on sensory details like the aroma of the tea—you foster an environment where intuition can thrive. Embracing a calm and centered state enables readers to connect deeply with the leaves and their meanings.

Practicing visualization techniques can also enhance intuitive connection. As you observe the shapes formed by the tea leaves, close your eyes and picture the symbols in your mind. Consider the meanings of each shape as you visualize them; this mental engagement can evoke emotions and personal associations that guide your interpretations. Visualization helps bridge the gap between cognitive understanding and intuitive awareness, allowing for a more integrated approach to readings.

Recording insights immediately after each reading is another valuable tool for reinforcing intuition. Using resources like Emacs to document your observations—including the symbols, your interpretations, and the emotions present during the reading—creates a comprehensive record of your journey with the tea leaves. Over time, revisiting past readings and reflecting on your growth encourages deeper connections with your intuitive insights. This process cultivates confidence in your ability to interpret—and trust—the messages revealed during the readings.

Additionally, engaging in group readings can facilitate the harnessing of intuition. Participating in collaborative settings allows readers to share their interpretations and insights, leading to increased familiarity with symbols and their meanings. Group dynamics encourage open dialogue, fostering a supportive atmosphere where collective energy nurtures intuitive exploration. Embracing diverse perspectives can further enhance one's understanding, providing an opportunity to learn from the varied experiences of fellow practitioners.

Lastly, allow for flexibility in your interpretation process. While symbols often carry traditional meanings, trusting your instincts requires an openness to subjective interpretations. Each reading is a personal experience, and the meanings behind the shapes can differ based on one's emotional landscape and life circumstances. Embrace the idea that intuition is a living force—one that evolves as readers engage with tea leaves and reflect on their journeys.

In conclusion, harnessing intuition in tea leaf readings is a dynamic and rewarding aspect of the practice that invites practitioners to explore the depths of their emotional landscapes and enhance their understanding of the symbols present in the leaves. By cultivating mindfulness, practicing visualization, recording insights, engaging with others, and allowing for flexibility in interpretations, readers can deepen their connection to tea leaf reading and enrich their interpretations. This journey of harnessing intuition ultimately transforms tea leaf reading into a profound tool for self-exploration and growth, revealing the wisdom contained in the shapes formed by tea leaves— a whisper of insight waiting to unfold with each cup.

14.2. Analytical Tools to Boost Interpretation Skills

In the realm of tea leaf reading, analytical tools serve as vital companions that enhance the practitioner's ability to interpret the intricate shapes and symbols formed in the cup. By incorporating structured methodologies that leverage technology, readers can heighten their analytical thinking and refine their interpretive skills, ultimately leading to deeper insights and a more rewarding practice.

To begin with, employing Emacs as a digital tool enables practitioners to document their readings systematically. This documentation process can encompass a variety of aspects, including the type of tea used, the specific symbols observed, and the context in which the reading takes place. By creating structured templates within Emacs, readers can document their entries in a coherent and organized manner, allowing them to refer back to past readings for comparative analysis. This systematic approach serves to solidify readers' understanding of how specific shapes relate to their lives, heightening their analytical acumen over time.

Building on this structure, practitioners can enhance their interpretation skills by incorporating analytical frameworks to evaluate their readings. For example, readers could adopt a method of categorizing symbols based on emotional resonance, life themes, or contextual relevance. By creating these categories within their Emacs files, practitioners not only gain clarity in their interpretations but can also track recurring symbols and their meanings across multiple readings. This categorization process invites practitioners to explore patterns within their tea leaf readings, fostering a more intricate understanding of how these symbols interact with their lives.

Additionally, analytical tools can facilitate visual representations of tea leaf readings, empowering readers to create diagrams or flowcharts that map out the relationships between symbols. By employing graphical elements, practitioners can visually analyze their interpretations, uncovering nuanced connections that may not have been evident through text alone. This multidimensional approach to analysis enhances the reader's ability to engage with the tea leaves actively, stimulating creativity in their interpretations while providing a holistic view of the narratives expressed within each cup.

As practitioners immerse themselves in the practice, it is also valuable to engage in group discussions or workshops focused on analytical techniques. Sharing insights with fellow tea leaf readers can foster a collaborative learning environment where practitioners collectively evaluate the effectiveness of their interpretations. This dialogue often leads to deeper explorations of symbols, allowing for the incorporation of diverse perspectives that challenge preconceived notions or biases.

Training the analytical mind can also dovetail nicely with developing intuition. Engaging in exercises that focus on honing both analytical skills and intuitive responses can be a powerful practice. For instance, paired exercises that require one reader to articulate the meanings of observed shapes while another reader reflects intuitively on the same symbols promote a balance between analytical rigor and emotional resonance. This dual approach fosters resilience, adaptability, and mutual learning in the art of tasseography.

Furthermore, practitioners may experiment with different tea blends and their associated meanings as a means of analytical exploration. The exploration of how specific tea types influence the shapes formed can add layers of complexity to interpretations. Analyzing patterns that emerge from different teas not only enhances understanding but also invites a scientific curiosity that further fuels the reader's relationship with the craft.

Ultimately, the application of analytical tools within tea leaf reading enriches the overall practice, offering practitioners not only a systematic method of documentation but also a framework for deepening their interpretations. By combining technology, visual representations, group discussions, and exercises that promote analytical and intuitive skills, practitioners cultivate a richer understanding of tasseography that honors the tradition while embracing innovative methodologies.

As readers journey through their tea leaf reading experiences, the analytical tools employed serve as a compass guiding them toward deeper insights and self-discovery. With each reading documented in structured formats, interpreted with clarity, and analyzed with creativity, practitioners unveil the wisdom waiting patiently within each cup of tea, ultimately enhancing their connection to the art of tasseography.

14.3. Exercises to Cultivate Insight

In the realm of tea leaf reading, exercises to cultivate insight hold immense potential for practitioners seeking to deepen their understanding of this ancient art. These exercises encourage readers to explore their intuition, enhance their interpretative skills, and develop personal connections with the symbols revealed by tea leaves. Integrating a range of reflective practices can transform the reading experience into a profound journey of self-discovery, allowing individuals to embrace the wisdom contained within each cup.

One of the first exercises involves mindful observation, which encourages practitioners to cultivate a sense of presence and attention during readings. Before engaging with the tea leaves, readers can take a few moments to ground themselves in the present. Close your eyes, take a few deep breaths, and visualize the space around you. Allow thoughts to flow freely without attachment, fostering a calm and conducive environment for tea leaf reading. Once centered, proceed to observe the shapes formed by the tea leaves with heightened awareness. Reflect on your emotional reactions to the symbols, noting how they resonate within you.

Engaging in a "symbol exploration" exercise can further enhance interpretation skills. After completing a reading, practitioners can select a specific shape that stood out to them and delve into its meanings. Using resources like Emacs, document personal interpretations, cultural associations, and emotional responses tied to that symbol. Over time, readers will build a deeper understanding of the nuances of each symbol, allowing for richer interpretations during future readings.

In addition to working with symbols, creative visualization exercises can help facilitate insight. After consuming the tea and turning the cup, readers might visualize the leaves forming various shapes. Instead of focusing solely on their actual positions, envision what these shapes represent in the context of your life. This imaginative engagement with the symbols invites practitioners to explore their emotional landscapes, fostering personal connections with the insights derived from the leaves.

Collaboration with fellow practitioners offers another valuable opportunity to cultivate insight. Organizing group readings where participants interpret the same cup can lead to enlightening conversations. Each person's unique perspective may reveal new dimensions of understanding, encouraging an exploration of collective meanings and enriching the traditional practices of tasseography. After such sessions, readers can engage in reflective discussions, fostering a deeper appreciation for diverse interpretations and the rich tapestry of tea leaf reading.

Keeping a dedicated tea leaf reading journal enhances self-reflection and insight cultivation. Embrace a structured approach by documenting each reading's date, type of tea used, observations, and interpretations. Use Emacs to categorize readings thematically or symbolically, creating pathways to sift through past insights easily. Revisiting these recorded experiences allows practitioners to trace their growth over time, reinforcing the connection between past readings and present circumstances.

Finally, encourage practitioners to allow room for ambiguity and uncertainty in their readings. Not every interpretation needs to yield clear or easily discernible insights. Embracing the unfolding nature of the practice promotes mindfulness and nurtures a spirit of curiosity. Reflect on reading experiences that may have felt inconclusive but bore reflections that evolved later. It invites practitioners to remain patient with the process, knowing that tea leaf reading is inherently fluid and ties closely to individual experiences.

Through these exercises to cultivate insight, practitioners of tea leaf reading can build their intuitive capacities and deepen their connection to the symbols present in every cup. By engaging fully with their readings, utilizing collaborative opportunities, and maintaining a strong reflective practice, individuals embrace the essence of tasseography as a dynamic journey of personal growth and understanding. Each session with tea leaves becomes an invitation to explore the mysteries of life, ultimately guiding readers toward deeper insights and self-awareness that enrich their journeys of discovery.

14.4. Documenting Personal Growth

Documenting personal growth through the practice of tea leaf reading, or tasseography, serves as a powerful means of reflection and self-discovery. This process not only allows practitioners to track their progress over time but also encourages them to engage deeply with their intuition and the diverse meanings that emerge from the symbols formed by tea leaves. By utilizing structures and methods conducive to growth, readers become more attuned to the narratives their readings unveil, reinforcing the inherent value of this ancient art.

To begin the journey of documentation, practitioners can create a system that captures key aspects of their readings, including the date, the type of tea used, the symbols observed, and the personal interpretations that arise. This systematic approach ensures that readers have a comprehensive record of their experiences, facilitating reflection on how their understanding of symbols evolves. Tools such as Emacs can enhance this process, allowing users to create structured templates that organize information in accessible ways, enabling quick reference to past readings and insights.

As readers continue to document their tea leaf readings, it is essential to create a dedicated space for reflection—a journal or digital platform where one can articulate thoughts and feelings about each reading. This space can serve as a repository of personal growth, revealing patterns of emotions and experiences that resonate with the shapes formed in their cups. By regularly revisiting this journal, practitioners can gain clarity on how their interpretations shift over time, reinforcing their connection to both the symbols and their own personal journeys.

Incorporating personal reflections into the documentation process is vital. After each reading, readers can take a moment to write about their emotional responses and the life events or circumstances that inform their interpretations. This practice emphasizes the concept that each tea leaf reading is not simply a moment of prophecy but rather an exploration of the individual's inner world and external realities. By naming those feelings and experiences, practitioners can create a tapestry of personal insights that deepens their understanding of the art.

Additionally, practitioners can set specific goals or themes for their tea leaf readings, allowing for focused exploration. For example, a reader might dedicate a month to exploring themes of self-love or career transitions, and then use subsequent readings to pull insights related to these areas. Documenting these targeted readings offers a concrete way of observing shifts and changes in one's life, reinforcing the dynamic relationship between the tea leaves and the emotions they invoke.

Moreover, practitioners should not shy away from documenting readings that feel ambiguous or unclear. Every reading, whether straightforward or perplexing, holds value in the learning process. By embracing these vagueness, readers can reflect on what uncertainties arise, and how those uncertainties might align with their life situations. This practice cultivates resilience, encouraging honesty and vulnerability in one's relationship with both the symbols and themselves.

Participating in workshops or community readings can additionally enhance the documentation process. Engaging with other practitioners not only offers the opportunity to share interpretations but enables readers to gain insights into how various individuals approach similar symbols. Together, the shared experience fosters a sense of belonging and reflection that enriches not only individual journeys but also the community as a whole. When documenting insights collaboratively or discussing them in group settings, practitioners amplify their understanding of their readings.

Ultimately, documenting personal growth through tea leaf readings promotes a deeper appreciation and understanding of both the practice of tasseography and the complexities of the self. By embracing organization, mindful reflection, shared learning, and goal-oriented focuses, practitioners cultivate a meaningful journey that connects them to the symbols in their tea leaves and the stories they reveal. This process transforms tea leaf readings into a dynamic dialogue with one's own intuition, inviting endless exploration, learning, and personal discovery on the path ahead.

14.5. Blending Creativity with Codification

Blending creativity with codification within tea leaf reading represents an exciting journey where the ancient practices of tasseography can be enhanced through modern interpretations and systematic organization. As practitioners navigate the intricate world of interpreting shapes formed by tea leaves, integrating artistic expression with structured methodologies can transform the reading experience, enriching both insights and personal connections to the symbols found in each cup.

To start, practitioners can craft a personalized divination toolkit that combines traditional elements of tasseography with innovative tools suited to their unique styles. This toolkit can include items that resonate with the individual, such as specific tea blends that hold special significance, a carefully selected teacup that enhances the visual aspects of the reading, and materials for documenting interpretations. By thoughtfully curating the tools they use, practitioners create an environment that fosters creativity and inspiration, encouraging deeper engagement with the reading process.

Incorporating art and creativity into tea leaf readings allows for expressive interpretations that transcend conventional meanings. Practitioners can embrace artistic elements by sketching the shapes revealed by the tea leaves, using colors and intricate designs to express the emotions and narratives tied to each reading. This creative exercise elevates the symbolism in tea leaf reading, inviting readers to explore their unique perspectives and relationships with the shapes formed by the leaves.

For those inclined towards DIY projects, creating customized items that enhance the practice can also enrich the experience. This could involve crafting a personal journal specifically designed for logging tea leaf readings, complete with prompts for reflection and sections for sketches or visual representations. Alternatively, practitioners might create a symbol dictionary that integrates their own insights alongside traditional meanings, blending creativity with codification in a tangible resource. Such personalized projects enable readers to engage with their tea leaf practice in a way that reflects their individuality and journey.

Using Emacs enhances the blending of creativity and codification by providing a versatile platform for managing readings, documenting insights, and analyzing patterns over time. Within Emacs, practitioners can create structured documents that incorporate both templates for readings and spaces for personal reflections, allowing distinct voices to emerge through their interpretations. This integration of technology empowers practitioners to maintain organized records while fostering creativity, enabling them to visualize their journeys through tea leaf reading and capture the nuances of their experiences.

The combination of artistry and precision in the practice of tea leaf reading encourages practitioners to embrace the beauty of both intuition and analytical skills. While the shapes formed by the tea leaves invite emotional engagement, the codification process—through organized documentation and reflective journaling—offers a grounding framework. This harmonious balance enhances the depth of insights practitioners derive from their readings, ultimately leading to a more profound understanding of the symbols and their meanings.

In essence, blending creativity with codification enhances the practice of tea leaf reading by encouraging personal expression and fostering an organized approach to interpretation. Embracing this duality empowers practitioners to honor the traditions of tasseography while adapting to contemporary contexts, ultimately deepening their connection to the art and its significance in their lives. As practitioners continue to explore the intersections of creativity and codification within their tea leaf reading journeys, they will uncover not just the wisdom within their cups but also a greater appreciation for the transformative nature of this ancient practice.

15. Creative Tools for 'Reading' Exercises

15.1. Crafting a Personalized Divination Toolkit

Crafting a personalized divination toolkit is a fulfilling venture for those looking to deepen their experience in tea leaf reading, also known as tasseography. A tailored toolkit not only enhances the overall practice but also imbues it with personal significance and intention. This section will delve into the elements and considerations that can help practitioners create a meaningful and effective set of tools, unifying tradition and individual expression.

To begin with, the cornerstone of any divination toolkit is the tea itself. Consider the types of tea you will use during your readings. Each variety brings unique flavors, aromas, and symbolic associations to the process. For instance, black tea, with its robust and grounding qualities, may serve those seeking clarity in challenging situations, while green tea is often favored for its refreshing and revitalizing properties, inviting new beginnings. Choosing a select few teas that resonate with your intentions can enrich your readings, providing a harmonious foundation for the reflective journey ahead.

Next, one of the most critical elements of your toolkit is the teacup or vessel used for readings. The choice of cup can greatly influence the reading experience. Consider selecting a vessel that feels aesthetically pleasing and comfortable to hold. Porcelain cups are a traditional favorite, providing smooth surfaces that easily reveal the formed shapes, while glass cups can offer a visual appreciation of the tea leaves as they swirled during brewing. Engaging with your cup, both visually and tactilely, helps establish a deeper connection with the reading process, encouraging mindfulness and focus.

In addition to tea and cups, adding specific utensils to your toolkit can further enhance your readings. For instance, a dedicated infuser or strainer allows for better control over how tea is brewed while mini-mizing debris. This simple inclusion not only improves the sensory experience but ensures that the leaves settle appropriately in the cup for desirable reading patterns. Furthermore, consider tools for jotting down interpretations—be it a beautiful journal or utilizing digital resources like Emacs. Setting up a system for easy documentation is crucial, allowing you to capture insights seamlessly during or after readings.

Beyond practical tools, infusing your toolkit with elements of art and creativity can enrich the experience as well. Consider adding a sketchbook or a set of colored pencils to illustrate the shapes and symbols you observe during readings. Engaging in visual representation fosters a deeper connection to the tea leaves and allows for expression beyond words. You may wish to create a 'symbol dictionary' where sketches can accompany the meanings you interpret. This blending of visual artistry with tradition enhances the richness of your practice, offering new pathways for understanding.

Furthermore, breathing life into your toolkit with personal ritual items can infuse meaning into your readings. Items such as crystals, feathers, or even candles can serve as focal points for intention-setting. Establishing a ritualistic element can enhance the tea leaf reading practice, instilling it with a sense of sacredness. For instance, lighting a candle before reading can mark the transition from daily life to the sacred space of divination, beckoning an invitation to engage deeply with the insights that arise.

As you reflect on your personalization efforts, consider the well-being of your reading space. Create an inviting environment equipped with soft lighting and calming scents—perhaps from incense or essential oils—that soothe the senses and cultivate a tranquil atmosphere conducive to tea leaf reading. This intentional environment reinforces mindfulness, allowing you to engage fully with your tea leaves and the ritual surrounding them.

Finally, the act of crafting your personalized divination toolkit itself is imbued with meaning. This endeavor encourages you to reflect on your journey, values, and intentions as a practitioner. Each element contributes to your experience as a tea leaf reader in unique ways, allowing you to blend tradition with personal expression.

In conclusion, creating a personalized divination toolkit for tea leaf reading involves thoughtfully selecting items that resonate with your intentions and experiences. By curating your teas, choosing an appropriate cup, adding essential utensils, infusing artistic elements, and creating a nurturing reading environment, you set the stage for a deeply engaging practice. This toolkit will serve as a companion as you delve into the enchanting world of tea leaves, guiding your journey of self-discovery and insight. Embrace the opportunity to blend artistry with tradition, crafting a reflective practice that celebrates the wisdom found within each cup.

15.2. Incorporating Art and Creativity

In the world of tea leaf reading, creativity serves as an essential element that enhances the experience and interpretation process. By incorporating art into the practice, readers are not only able to enrich their connection with the symbols present in the leaves but can also infuse their personal interpretations with energy and expression. This synergy between artistry and tea leaf reading invites practitioners to explore the nuanced meanings hidden within these symbols, expanding their journey into a rich tapestry of personal discovery and insight.

One approach to integrating creativity into the tea leaf reading practice is through artistic representations of the shapes formed by the leaves. This can be a delightful and engaging exercise that allows readers to draw or paint the symbols they observe in their cups. By visualizing these shapes, practitioners cultivate a deeper connection to the meanings they interpret. Art serves as a medium that encourages exploration beyond words, capturing the essence of symbols in a literal and metaphorical sense. These artistic renditions can later be used in journaling practices, enhancing reflective documentation of readings by providing visual context that illustrates the meanings associated with different shapes.

Another avenue for fostering creativity involves creating dedicated spaces for tea reading that are infused with playful and artistic elements. Practitioners might customize their reading environments by introducing colors, textures, and décor that align with their personal aesthetic. This could include painted backgrounds, dreamcatchers, or inspirational quotes that resonate with the themes they wish to explore in their readings. The physical arrangement reinforces a playful atmosphere that encourages freedom of thought, enabling the practitioners to approach the tea leaf reading with imagination and openness.

Building on this, creating a DIY toolkit that combines traditional tea reading tools with customized items serves to enhance both artistry and practicality. For example, practitioners may choose to craft their tea vessels, creating unique cups that bear personal symbolism or artistic motifs. Moreover, incorporating handmade notebooks or journals designed specifically to document interpretations allows readers to combine their artistic expression with their tea leaf reading documentation. These customized tools not only honor the traditional aspects of the practice but also amplify the reader's individuality, offering a personalized connection to their art.

The integration of technology within creative practices also offers thrilling possibilities. Using platforms like Emacs, practitioners can design collaborative documents that include sketches, written interpretations, and shared insights. This dynamic interplay of creativity and organization allows for a rich dialogue to unfold around the meanings derived from tea leaves. Readers may even experiment with coding functions in Emacs that prompt artistic responses based on symbols encountered—inviting an interplay between intuitive thought and creative expression.

Additionally, engaging with fellow readers in community workshops can serve as a fertile ground for cultivating creativity. These gatherings provide opportunities for practitioners to share their artistic interpretations and engage in collaborative exercises. Group readings often lead to the exploration of collective symbolism, where individuals gain insight by comparing their interpretations, linking their shared experiences to the narratives emerging from the leaves. This communal aspect fosters an enriching environment that celebrates creativity while reinforcing the societal ties that confront the solitary nature of individual readings.

As readers engage artistically with their tea leaf practice, they also nurture their intuition and emotional resonance. Creativity encourages individuals to express their feelings freely, leading to interpretations that are nuanced and deeply rooted in personal experience. By recognizing that both creativity and emotion are integral components of the tea leaf reading experience, practitioners enhance their interpretive skills while honoring the sacred storytelling aspect of tasseography.

In summary, incorporating art and creativity into tea leaf reading enriches the interpretative process, enhances personal engagement, and nurtures self-discovery. By embracing the connections between creativity, tradition, and technology, practitioners can delve into a dynamic journey that celebrates both the mysteries of the tea leaves and the richness of their personal narratives. This exploration encourages readers to view the practice of tasseography as a living art form that evolves with each cup, inviting them to unlock deeper insights and express the stories woven within the leaves.

15.3. DIY Projects for Customized Tools

In the world of tea leaf reading, or tasseography, the practice of customizing tools can significantly enhance the reading experience while allowing practitioners to infuse their personalities and preferences into the art. This custom approach fosters a deeper connection with the tea leaves and the insights they reveal. In this section, we explore various DIY projects that enable tea leaf readers to create personalized tools, enhancing both their practice and enjoyment of the art.

To begin, one of the most impactful DIY projects involves crafting a personalized tea leaves journal. This unique journal not only serves as a record of previous readings and interpretations but also allows practitioners to integrate their artistic expressions. Readers can choose to design the journal cover creatively, using colors, motifs, or images that resonate with them. The pages inside can be divided into sections, accommodating different teas, symbols, notes, and insights gained from readings. This personalized journal enhances the tea leaf reading experience by inviting practitioners to document their encounters intimately, fostering memory retention and reinforcing learning through reflection.

Additionally, custom teacups can be both functional and symbolic. Practitioners can select a teacup that reflects their aesthetic or design one that incorporates personal symbols or imagery significant to them. This teacup becomes not only a vessel for brewing but also an integral part of the reading, infusing each session with meaning. Personalizing a cup allows readers to create an emotional attachment to their practice, providing an anchor that enhances feelings of enjoyment and mindfulness during the ritual.

Another significant DIY project involves creating a symbol chart or poster that visually represents the shapes commonly encountered during readings. This chart can serve as a reference guide for new practitioners and a source of inspiration for seasoned readers. With creativity at the forefront, practitioners can hand-draw or print images of common symbols alongside their interpretations and meanings. This engaging approach allows them to grasp the symbolic language inherent in tea leaf reading better while ensuring that they remain linked to the richer history of the art.

Some practitioners may also consider developing an oracle box, comprised of various tools directly related to tea leaf reading. This box could include tea samples, small containers for loose leaves, infusers, a measuring spoon for precision, and crystals or charms that connect with the energies they wish to channel during readings. Each element in the box can be chosen for its specific significance and contribution to the reading experience. As readers explore their oracle boxes, they develop a sense of ritual and intentionality, reinforcing the sacred nature of the practice.

Utilizing resources like Emacs to document how each of these tools impacts readings can deepen one's understanding and ability to assess what works best for them. Readers can set up their Emacs environment to include sections for reflections on how the custom tools enhance or change their interpretation experience. Documenting changes over time allows for meaningful insights into the evolution of their tea leaf readings, empowering practitioners to refine their methods continuously.

Moreover, collaborative workshops can serve as excellent venues for sharing DIY ideas and techniques. Engaging with fellow tea leaf readers in a group setting encourages creativity while nurturing a sense of community. Participants can exchange ideas, share their personalized tools, and inspire one another creatively. This collaborative spirit fosters growth, innovation, and connection among practitioners —each enriching the practice as a whole.

In conclusion, customizing tools for tea leaf reading through DIY projects invites practitioners to engage wholly with both the process and the art of tasseography. By creating personalized journals, crafting unique teacups, designing symbol charts, and developing oracle boxes, readers enrich their experiences with meaning and creativity. These customized elements not only enhance reflection and connection during readings but also contribute to a greater sense of identity within the practice. Embracing customization ultimately deepens the bond between practitioners and their craft, making each cup of tea a journey not just through the leaves but through the personal stories and expressions vibrant within each reader's life.

15.4. Using Emacs for Dynamic Interpretation

Using Emacs for Dynamic Interpretation provides a compelling intersection between the timeless practice of tea leaf reading, or tasseography, and the robust functionality of Emacs—an extensible text editor known for its customization and versatility. This dynamic synthesis of technology and tradition empowers practitioners to delve deeper into the interpretations of symbols formed by tea leaves, enhancing both the analytical and intuitive aspects of the practice. By utilizing Emacs effectively, readers can elevate their tea leaf reading experiences, allowing for a more fluid and organized approach to capturing insights and reflections.

One of the most distinctive features of Emacs is its ability to create custom workflows tailored to individual reading styles. Practitioners can begin by setting up an environment that encourages focused documentation. For instance, creating an Org mode file specifically for tea leaf readings provides a structured way to log each session's details, including the type of tea used, symbols observed, personal interpretations, and emotional associations. This systematic approach not only organizes the data but also helps reinforce the understanding of recurring themes and symbols, paving the way for personal growth and deeper insights over time.

To further enhance the reading experience, Emacs can be used to create interactive tools that engage both mind and intuition. By developing simple scripts or functions, practitioners can automate tasks such as generating prompt questions related to specific readings or enabling random selection of themes to explore for their next session. This playful interaction invites curiosity and nurtures an exploratory spirit in deciphering the mysteries of tea leaves. The adaptability of Emacs supports a dynamic environment where creativity and logic merge seamlessly, fostering a balanced approach to interpretations.

Moreover, Emacs provides an ideal space for collaborative efforts within the tea leaf reading community. Practitioners can share insights through a shared repository of interpretations, with each member contributing to a living document that evolves with time. The collaborative aspect encourages discussions around symbols, emotions, and personal stories, enriching the understanding of tea leaf readings while fostering connections among practitioners. By maintaining a digital platform for this exchange, Emacs cultivates an inclusive environment where individuals can learn from one another and refine their practices collectively.

Incorporating visual elements into the Emacs environment also enhances tea leaf reading. Readers can create graphical representations of the shapes observed in their cups, allowing for a visual analysis that complements textual interpretations. This dynamic blending of art and precision invites practitioners to engage deeply with the leaves and nurture their intuitive skills. By illustrating shapes, practitioners can foster an emotional connection to their readings, providing insights that might elude purely verbal interpretations.

As practitioners become more adept at using Emacs, they might also explore integrating their digital readings with broader themes related to personal journeys. For instance, utilizing Emacs' capabilities to tag entries based on emotional states or thematic elements can unveil patterns, revelations, or areas requiring attention. Analyzing these connections can empower readers to make informed life choices and engage more thoughtfully with their daily experiences.

Ultimately, using Emacs for dynamic interpretation in tea leaf reading is about fostering a harmonious relationship between technology and tradition. By creating a personalized, adaptable environment for documenting and reflecting on readings, practitioners not only deepen their understanding of the shapes formed by tea leaves but also illuminate their paths toward self-discovery. This synthesis empowers practitioners to be both the recipients and the creators of meaning, unveiling the wealth of wisdom that tea leaf reading offers.

As practitioners embark on this explorative journey, they embrace the potential for growth and personal insight through the lens of both technology and the mystical art of tasseography. With Emacs serving as a steadfast companion, readers unlock the power within each cup, allowing their intuitive journeys to flourish as they navigate the intersection of old and new, art and analysis, creativity and codification.

15.5. Combining Artistry and Precision

In the mesmerizing realm of tea leaf reading, a delicate balance exists between artistry and precision, intertwining the mystical art of tasseography with the structured capabilities of technology. This symbiosis invites practitioners to explore their intuitive abilities while harnessing rational thought, creating a unique space where creativity flourishes alongside methodical interpretation. The combination of these elements enhances the reading experience, transforming each session into a profound journey of personal insight.

At the heart of this blend lies the understanding that tea leaf reading serves not only as a means of divination but also as a canvas for self-expression. Practitioners fold artistry into their readings by infusing creative elements into their ritual. This may involve sketching the symbols observed or compiling visual diaries that reflect personal interpretations. The act of merging artistry with the traditional shapes allows readers to deepen their emotional engagement, illuminating meanings that may expand beyond conventional interpretations. This creative expression transforms the reading into a tangible narrative—one that resonates with the reader's emotions and experiences.

However, artistry alone does not define the richness of tea leaf reading. Equally vital is the precision that accompanies interpreting the shapes formed by the leaves. Each symbol carries established meanings that offer insight into the querent's circumstances, guiding practitioners through life's complexities. Readers who master the lexicon of traditional symbols can interweave their knowledge with intuition, creating a nuanced tapestry of interpretations that captivate the heart and mind. Precision becomes a grounding tool, enabling practitioners to extract meaning from even the simplest shapes and relate them to the broader themes of life.

Emacs serves as a bridge between this artistry and precision, allowing readers to document their insights systematically while nurturing creative expression. Through customized templates and structured organization, practitioners can catalog their interpretations, refer back to past readings, and recognize the patterns that emerge over time. By meshing the creative aspects of their tea leaf practice with the analytical capabilities of Emacs, readers foster an environment that reverberates with personal significance, enhancing the depth of their interactions with the leaves.

Moreover, the course of tea leaf reading evolves when practitioners participate in community-based exploration. Engaging with fellow readers through workshops, forums, or collaborative projects creates a dynamic landscape where artistry and precision intersect. Group discussions encourage sharing diverse interpretations, enriching individual experiences by revealing new dimensions, and fostering a deeper contextual understanding of symbols that may challenge traditional narratives. This community aspect amplifies creativity, as collaborators inspire one another to approach readings with fresh perspectives, pushing the boundaries of conventional interpretations.

As technology continues to advance, readers are encouraged to blend innovative tools into their practices while respecting the core principles of tasseography. The incorporation of digital resources allows for flexibility in interpretation, giving practitioners the freedom to explore and redefine their understanding while honoring the emotional and cultural significance of the symbols encountered. Embracing a mindset of openness becomes crucial for readers navigating this balance; it allows them to move fluidly between analytical reasoning and intuitive insight.

Ultimately, the melding of artistry and precision in tea leaf reading allows practitioners to embark on a transformative journey that pays homage to tradition while embracing contemporary methods. As readers navigate the intertwining pathways of creativity and analytical thought, they unveil new meanings in their interpretations and foster a deeper connection with the symbols present in their tea leaves. In this exploration, tea leaf reading evolves from a simple ritual into a dynamic practice rich with insight, reflection, and personal growth—a journey where the tea leaves not only tell stories but inspire readers to become active participants in their narratives.

As you engage with this harmonious blend of artistry and precision, may you unlock the potential that resides within each cup of tea, embracing the wisdom carried by the leaves as you forge your own path through the poetic world of tasseography. Through this artistry and precision, you will find connections to your own experiences, illuminating avenues back into yourself and uncovering the magic that flows through each moment.

16. Navigating Life's Puzzles with Tea and Technology

16.1. Decoding Life Events with Symbolic Guidance

In tea leaf reading, known as tasseography, life events can often feel chaotic, unpredictable, or overwhelming. As practitioners of this enchanting art delve into the symbolic shapes and patterns formed by the tea leaves remaining in their cups, they uncover a form of guidance that can illuminate their personal journeys. In this chapter, we will explore how to decode life events using symbolic guidance from tea leaf readings, empowering readers to transform uncertainty into clarity, and navigate their paths with confidence and purpose.

The journey begins with the act of preparing for a tea leaf reading. Setting intentions is vital; practitioners may reflect on specific life events, emotions, or concerns they wish to explore. This clear focus establishes a framework for interpretation, helping readers remain attuned to the messages communicated by the tea leaves. In the quiet moment before the reading begins, readers should ground themselves, creating a space that fosters openness to insights that may arise during the experience.

Once the tea has settled, practitioners begin to investigate the shapes formed by the leaves. Each symbol can provide a piece of the puzzle, acting as a metaphor for the life events or emotions that permeate the querent's existence. For instance, a circle may reflect wholeness or completion, suggesting that a chapter in life is drawing to a close, while an anchor might signify stability and the need to stay grounded amid tumultuous experiences. As readers engage with these symbols, they cultivate the trust necessary to decipher the hidden meanings linked to their personal circumstances.

Interpreting the symbols involves combining traditional meanings with the practitioner's emotional responses and experiences. It is important to recognize that while common shapes carry established interpretations, the meanings can shift based on individual contexts. This adaptability requires readers to remain present, allowing their intuitive insights to drive their understanding. By considering how specific shapes resonate with their own life experiences, practitioners cultivate a deeper connection with the tea leaves and the wisdom they offer.

Through the exploration of tea leaf symbols, practitioners can decode life events that may evoke feelings of uncertainty or confusion. For example, if a practitioner observes a serpent shape in their reading, this could signal transformation and healing—encouraging the reader to consider how they can embrace change or release old patterns that no longer serve them. Identifying these connections between symbols and personal experiences allows for a transformative reading that encourages self-reflection and growth.

Furthermore, it is helpful to maintain a diligent record of readings undertaken, whether in a journal or within a digital platform like Emacs. Documenting the interpretations, patterns, and emotional responses surrounding each reading serves as a tangible connection to the journey undertaken. Over time, readers can revisit past readings to observe how symbols arc across their lives, revealing patterns that may inform present and future choices. This retrospective analysis promotes clarity, increases coherence in interpreting symbols, and can create a roadmap for navigating forthcoming events.

Engaging in collaborative workshops or community discussions enhances the exploration of life events through tea leaf readings. By sharing readings with others and offering diverse perspectives, practitioners discover that symbols often resonate on multiple levels, illuminating insights that may not have been apparent individually. This exchange nurtures a collective atmosphere where learning flourishes, and readers can assess their interpretations against alternate viewpoints, ultimately expanding their understanding and interpretation skills.

As readers cultivate their intuitive skills and adaptive abilities, tea leaf reading emerges as a robust guiding practice that aids in decoding life events. By acknowledging the symbols formed by the leaves, engaging in reflective documentation, and fostering a sense of community, practitioners can transform unclear and complex situations into actionable insights.

In conclusion, decoding life events with symbolic guidance offers a powerful avenue for self-discovery and growth through tea leaf reading. By engaging thoughtfully with the shapes produced by the leaves, practitioners unlock personal narratives and opportunities for reflection that can serve as guideposts in navigating their journeys. As readers embrace the rich language of tea leaves with openness, they illuminate the pathways ahead—finding clarity amid chaos and transforming uncertainty into purpose. Tea leaf readings empower individuals to decode their life events—revealing the wisdom that lies within, waiting to be uncovered through the intricate dance of leaves in their cups.

16.2. Symbolic Journeys Through Personal History

In examining the journey of personal history through the symbolic language of tea leaves, one finds a remarkable intersection of past experiences, current emotions, and future possibilities. In tea leaf reading, or tasseography, symbols formed by the residual leaves serve as mirrors reflecting the querent's life narrative, unveiling insights that resonate with their unique experiences. By engaging thoughtfully with the shapes and formations, practitioners can decode aspects of their personal history, weaving a deeper understanding of themselves and their journeys.

At the core of this exploration is the understanding that every symbol encountered in a reading is steeped in personal significance. For instance, a shape resembling an eye may invoke memories of intuition or perceptions that have shaped one's life decisions. Alternatively, a crescent moon may invite reflection on cycles of growth or shifts in emotional states, reminding readers of the ebb and flow inherent in their life stories. As readers interpret these symbols, they connect deeply to the narratives embedded within their cups, gaining insights into how past events have defined their present circumstances.

Practitioners can enhance this process by documenting their reflections in journaling practices, potentially utilizing tools like Emacs to create structured entries that capture both insights and emotions relating to each reading. By recording their interpretations, practitioners build a richer tapestry of their personal history, tracing the threads of symbolism that recur over time. This practice serves as a powerful reminder of past moments and lessons learned, illuminating the interconnectedness of experiences and emotions while offering guidance for future paths.

The relationship between the symbols and personal history can also manifest in the patterns observed across multiple readings. As practitioners engage with tea leaf readings consistently, they may find that specific symbols repeatedly surface, indicating unresolved issues or recurring themes in their lives. This observation invites introspection, prompting practitioners to explore the meanings attached to these symbols more deeply. For example, if a practitioner frequently encounters a symbol representing a bridge, it could signify the need for connection or resolution in a relationship or project that has remained stagnant over time.

Moreover, engaging with the community of readers can amplify this exploration. Participating in group readings fosters a collaborative atmosphere where individuals can share their interpretations and connect with others' life experiences. Observations and reflections from fellow practitioners can illuminate blind spots, encouraging shared learning and growth within the community. Embracing diverse perspectives enriches one's understanding of symbols, inviting readers to see their personal histories from new angles and deepen their interpretations.

In parallel, practitioners are reminded that the journey through tea leaf reading is fluid; personal history is not static but rather an evolving narrative. Allowing for transformation from past experiences creates a lightness, enabling readers to reinterpret their relationship with symbols as they progress through different phases of life. This flexibility nurtures resilience, fostering a deeper understanding of how the past informs the present and shapes the future.

Ultimately, exploring personal history through the lens of tea leaves offers readers an invaluable opportunity to uncover layers of meaning and insight. By engaging thoughtfully with the symbols, documenting interpretations, and participating in community discussions, individuals can embark on a reflective journey that illuminates their past, enriches their present, and shapes their future. The beauty of tasseography lies in its ability to connect readers with their unique narratives, inviting them to unravel the complexities of their lives through the whispers and lessons hidden within the enigmatic shapes of tea leaves. In this way, practitioners not only decode the symbols of their personal history but also unveil the pathways toward a deeper understanding of themselves and their journey through life.

16.3. Alternative Pathways to Self-Knowledge

In the exploration of self-knowledge, alternative pathways can illuminate the complexities of personal discovery and understanding. Whether through the practical lens of tea leaf reading or the contemplative process of self-reflection, individuals are invited to engage with the myriad facets of their identities. This subchapter will delve into various avenues for self-knowledge that complement the art of tasseography, providing a richer tapestry of insights for practitioners as they navigate their journeys of growth and exploration.

Alternative pathways to self-knowledge can take many forms, encompassing a wide range of practices that guide individuals toward deeper introspection. One potent approach is the integration of creative expression, which often reveals hidden truths and insights that may lie beneath the surface. Engaging in activities such as journaling, painting, or even crafting can evoke emotional responses that promote self-awareness. These creative outlets serve as a means of externalizing thoughts and feelings, providing clarity on the complexities of one's inner world. Practitioners of tea leaf reading may find value in keeping a journal that combines both artistic expression and recorded readings, thus reinforcing their connection to the symbols while inviting exploration of their own narratives.

Another alternative pathway involves the exploration of mindfulness and meditation—a practice that encourages individuals to cultivate awareness of their thoughts, feelings, and bodily sensations. Practicing mindfulness fosters an environment conducive to reflection, allowing practitioners to assess their emotions and experiences without judgment. This introspective process can be particularly beneficial as individuals approach their tea leaf readings, helping them to clear their minds and create a focused space for interpreting the messages communicated by the tea leaves. Mindfulness exercises can be tailored to suit each individual's preferences, leading to deeper engagement with both the ritual of tea leaf reading and the symbols that unfold during readings.

Engaging with nature can also serve as a powerful avenue for self-discovery. Practitioners are encouraged to spend time outdoors, observing their surroundings and connecting with the natural world. Nature offers valuable insights into the cycles of life, renewal, and interconnectedness—elements that resonate with the symbolism in tea leaf reading. By immersing oneself in nature, individuals foster a sense of presence that can enhance their readings, allowing them to approach their tea leaves with a renewed perspective and receptivity.

Alternative pathways for self-knowledge can also extend into the realm of community engagement. Connecting with fellow practitioners of tasseography strengthens the ties between individuals who share a common interest in exploring symbolic interpretations. Engaging in discussions, attending workshops, or participating in group readings fosters an enriching learning environment where readers can enhance their skills and gain new perspectives. The collective wisdom arising from shared experiences empowers practitioners to view their personal journeys through diverse lenses, promoting a deeper understanding of their insights.

Additionally, spiritual practices that complement tea leaf reading—such as visualization, energy healing, or tarot readings—can further enrich one's journey of self-discovery. Each practice offers its own unique set of symbols and interpretations, broadening the pathways for exploring personal insights. By embracing multiple modalities for introspection, practitioners can access a wealth of knowledge that informs their tea leaf readings, yielding deeper, more nuanced interpretations of the shapes left behind in their cups.

Ultimately, alternative pathways to self-knowledge encourage practitioners to engage with the world around them creatively, mindfully, and communally. By embracing diverse modes of exploration, individuals deepen their understanding of themselves and their experiences, transforming tea leaf reading from a simple divinatory art into a multifaceted journey of personal growth and reflection. As practitioners weave together these varied threads of self-discovery, they unlock the potential for profound insights that transcend the leaves, illuminating the mysteries of their own lives in the process. Embracing these alternative pathways not only enriches the practice of tea leaf reading but also fosters a deeper connection to the self, the community, and the ever-evolving journey of life.

16.4. Combining Logic and Emotion in Readings

Combining logic and emotion in readings is a nuanced practice that adds depth and richness to the art of tea leaf reading, or tasseography. While the symbolic shapes formed by tea leaves offer a foundation for interpretation grounded in traditional meanings, the interplay of rational thought and emotional insight enhances the reader's ability to derive nuanced messages from each cup. This combination invites practitioners to engage both their analytical mind and their intuitive heart, fostering a holistic approach to tea leaf reading.

At its core, the analytical component of interpreting tea leaves involves recognizing established symbols and their meanings. Each shape not only conveys specific connotations but also resonates with the querent's life experiences, emotions, and context. To marry this analytical aspect with emotional insight, practitioners must cultivate awareness of the feelings that arise during the reading process. Observing how an emotional reaction—whether it be joy, fear, excitement, or uncertainty—may influence interpretations ensures that the reading remains interconnected with the human experience.

Practitioners can begin by engaging in active reflection before diving into interpretations. Taking a moment to acknowledge their emotions, readers may ask themselves how they feel about the reading atmosphere, the symbols forming in the cup, and any immediate thoughts that arise. This initial mindfulness sets the stage for combining logic and emotion effectively; it encourages practitioners to remain grounded while also allowing emotional currents to inform their interpretations.

As the reader begins to decode the symbols, they can apply a logical framework to analyze the meanings represented by the tea leaves. Understanding the cultural and traditional significances associated with common shapes—such as the key representing new opportunities or the crescent moon signaling intuition—establishes a foundation for interpretations. However, rather than solely relying on this analytical framework, readers should allow their emotional insights to guide them. For example, if a heart shape emerges, the reader might logically interpret it as a symbol of love, but the emotional associations could lead to an exploration of self-love, friendship, or familial relationships, depending on the querent's current situation.

Throughout the reading process, practicing flexibility becomes a vital skill. Embracing the notion that interpretations can evolve based on emotional insights fosters an adaptive mindset. Readers might find that specific symbols evoke unexpected associations that deviate from their predefined meanings. For instance, if a bird appears in the leaves, it could convey a sense of freedom or new beginnings for one individual, but may resonate as a call for communication for another. This fluidity encourages practitioners to remain attuned to the evolving narrative, weaving together analytical observations and emotional insights as the tea leaves unveil their stories.

Moreover, documenting readings in a structured manner can enhance the ability to combine logic and emotion over time. Using Emacs as a digital framework allows readers to maintain records of their interpretations, discerning patterns as they track both emotional responses and analytical insights. This documentation fosters a continuous dialogue between the two dimensions, where readers can revisit past entries, reflect on how emotions influenced their interpretations, and refine their understanding of the symbols as their practices mature.

Combining logic and emotion is not only about interpreting symbols but also involves considering the querent's context. Practitioners should approach readings with sensitivity and awareness of the individual's experiences, recognizing that their insights may hold different levels of significance for varying individuals. Establishing open communication during the reading process invites querents to share their perspectives and feelings, allowing for a more nuanced interpretation shaped by both the reader's rational analysis and emotional resonance with the symbols.

Lastly, fostering connections with fellow practitioners promotes collaboration in the exploration of combining logic and emotion in readings. Group discussions, workshops, and online forums create spaces for sharing experiences, insights, and diverse interpretations. Exchanging ideas around how emotional awareness influences logical interpretations can offer fresh perspectives that deepens both personal practices and collective understanding.

In summary, combining logic and emotion in tea leaf readings invites practitioners to explore the intricate interplay of analytical thought and emotional insight. By remaining open to the layers of meaning present in the symbols, cultivating self-awareness, and fostering connections with others, readers can enrich their interpretations while honoring the complexities of the human experience. This approach provides an opportunity to dig deeper—transforming each tea leaf reading into a multidimensional journey of discovery, allowing practitioners to uncover the wisdom encoded in the delicate dance of tea leaves within their cups.

16.5. Exploring the Paradox of Technology and Spirituality

In the contemporary landscape of spirituality and technology, the paradox of integrating modern tools within age-old practices presents itself as both an opportunity and a challenge. Drawing from the ancient art of tea leaf reading, or tasseography, we find ourselves at a fascinating intersection where intuition meets innovation. This delicate balance requires practitioners to navigate their relationships with technology while remaining grounded in the spiritual depth of traditional practices. As we explore the multifaceted dimensions of this paradox, it becomes evident that technology can serve as an ally in our quest for self-discovery and spiritual growth, provided we approach it with intentionality and reverence.

As practitioners of tea leaf reading increasingly turn to digital tools, they find themselves equipped with resources that enhance their interpretive abilities. Programs like Emacs highlight the benefits of technology, offering a structure to document readings with an ease that goes beyond conventional journaling methods. The acts of organizing thoughts, categorizing symbols, and reflecting on past experiences can be streamlined, giving readers the clarity needed to engage deeply with the symbols and their meanings. Emphasizing the role of technology in spiritual practices does not negate the inherent values of these ancient arts; rather, it fosters a landscape in which innovation breathes new life into tradition.

However, this relationship between technology and spirituality is not without its complexities. Traditionalists may question whether modern tools dilute the authenticity of the tea leaf reading experience, as they perceive the risks of distraction or depersonalization. A crucial aspect of maintaining courtesy to traditional practices lies in cultivating an awareness of one's intent when utilizing technology. By grounding oneself in the ritual and symbolism the leaves offer, practitioners can ensure that the emotional resonance and intuitive connections remain central to their explorations.

We arrive at an invitation for practitioners to adopt a mindset of adaptability. Emphasizing flexibility allows readers to blend innovative tools with spiritual practices in authentic ways. Instead of viewing technology and spirituality as opposing forces, practitioners can embrace the interplay between them, discovering ways to harmoniously incorporate tools that yield personal insights while honoring established rituals. As practitioners approach their readings with curiosity, remaining open to the unexpected, they can nurture the realization that technology can be a bridge to deeper understanding rather than a hindrance.

Collaboration within the community enhances the dialogue surrounding the integration of technology and spirituality. Engaging with fellow practitioners—whether through workshops, online forums, or group discussions—creates spaces for shared learning. Through these communities, individuals can explore the nuances of interpreting tea leaves while sharing insights about how modern tools have influenced their readings. The beauty of traversing this path together strengthens connections and fosters a sense of belonging inherent in spiritual practices.

In anticipation of future developments, we must recognize that the practice of tasseography continues to evolve, reflective of the changing dynamics of society. As tea leaf reading gains broader interest, the infusion of new interpretations and methodologies will unfold. Moving forward, it becomes increasingly essential for practitioners to remain vigilant stewards of tradition while welcoming innovation that complements their practice. As the landscape of tea leaf reading broadens to engage new audiences, its essence—the self-discovery and connection facilitated through symbols—will persist, weaving the timelessness of the craft into contemporary experiences.

Ultimately, exploring the paradox of technology and spirituality invites tea leaf readers to embark on a journey that balances the old and new, engages intuition and analysis, and cultivates gratitude for the wisdom revealed through tea leaves. By weaving together the deep-seated traditions of tasseography with adaptive strategies enabled by modern tools, practitioners can illuminate their paths of self-discovery and introspection. This process reinforces the understanding that tea leaf reading is not merely a practice of divination but also one of deep connection with oneself and the cosmic tapestry of experiences that shape life's journey.

As tea leaf readers embrace this profound integration of technology and spirituality, they invite a broader narrative—the ongoing exploration of symbolic guidance from tea leaves. The whispers of the leaves become an invitation to reflect, connect, and grow, creating pathways for profound insights and meaningful journeys in the art of tasseography.

17. The Future of Tasseography: From Tradition to Innovation

17.1. Celebrating Traditional Practitioners

In the rich tapestry of tasseography, 'Celebrating Traditional Practitioners' brings to the forefront the invaluable contributions of those who have upheld the practice of tea leaf reading through the ages. These traditional practitioners not only serve as custodians of the art but also embody the essence of a practice deeply rooted in cultural heritage, spirituality, and community. Recognizing and honoring their roles enriches the modern discourse surrounding tea leaf reading, weaving together the past with contemporary interpretations and ensuring the survival of this ancient art.

Traditional practitioners have preserved the wisdom of tea leaf reading, passing it down through generations. Their knowledge is steeped in rich cultural contexts, histories, and rituals that transform the act of reading tea leaves into a profound journey of self-discovery and insight. Many of these practitioners have become not just readers but storytellers, guiding their querents through a landscape of symbols that reflect both the individual and the collective human experience. By celebrating these practitioners, we acknowledge the legacy they provide and the ways in which they have forged connections to their communities, teaching others about the interpretations and emotional nuances tied to various shapes formed by tea leaves.

Traditionally, these practitioners have engaged in tea leaf readings within intimate settings—creating spaces where individuals could connect, share stories, and seek guidance. These rituals often fostered emotional resonance within the reading, allowing the querent to explore their lives through the lens of established symbols and shapes. The communal aspect of these gatherings nurtured bonds among participants, encouraging empathy and support while highlighting the significance of the practice in the broader social fabric.

As tea leaf reading evolves within the modern context, it is essential to honor the traditional practitioners who have laid the groundwork for contemporary interpretations. Their knowledge informs current practices, offering insights that resonate deeply with those seeking guidance today. The melding of tradition and innovation signifies the potential for growth and evolution in the practice, underscoring the rich layers that contribute to the symbolic language of tasseography.

To celebrate these traditional practitioners, it is important to actively share their stories and contributions in workshops, online discussions, and literature dedicated to tea leaf reading. By showcasing their wisdom, readers can cultivate a deeper appreciation for the historical significance, ensuring that the art remains vibrant while embracing new interpretations. Documenting and honoring their teachings helps ground modern practices in a rich heritage, energizing the practice as it continues to unfold.

Acknowledging the significance of traditional practitioners within the framework of tea leaf reading fosters a sense of continuity, reminding modern practitioners of the ancient wisdom contained within each cup of tea. As readers engage with this art form, their individual journeys become part of a larger narrative—a collective exploration of self, culture, and spirituality that transcends time, inviting all who partake to find their unique connections within this captivating practice. By honoring the past while paving the way for future innovations, the art of tea leaf reading can flourish as a meaningful expression of human experience, resilience, and introspection.

The celebration of traditional practitioners, therefore, instills a commitment to nurturing the foundational tenets of tea leaf reading even as we explore contemporary innovations. This dual approach secures the vitality of the practice, allowing both personal discovery and spiritual illumination to thrive in the stories told by the vibrant shapes of tea leaves that continue to spark conversations, insights, and connections.

17.2. Anticipating Future Trends in Technology

Anticipating Future Trends in Technology provides an intriguing lens through which practitioners of tea leaf reading, or tasseography, can envision the evolving relationship between this ancient practice and the rapid technological advancements of our time. As we delve deeper into the interactivity of modern tools and traditions, we see the potential for transformative changes that promise to enrich our reading experiences, boost community engagement, and create new modalities for understanding tea leaves.

One of the most significant future trends is the integration of artificial intelligence (AI) and machine learning with tea leaf reading. Imagine a scenario where AI algorithms analyze past readings to recognize patterns in symbols, generating insights based on vast datasets of past interpretations. This could empower practitioners by providing suggestions or contextual data supporting their readings. While the art of interpreting tea leaves fundamentally remains rooted in intuition and personal experience, the integration of AI could serve as a supplementary tool for practitioners seeking clarity or affirmation, enhancing their confidence in the interpretations they derive.

Furthermore, as digital interfaces become increasingly immersive, the potential for virtual and augmented reality (VR and AR) experiences in tea leaf reading opens captivating pathways for practitioners. Readers could use AR applications to superimpose visual aids over their readings, helping them visualize standard symbols and their common meanings as they interact with the leaves directly. Similarly, VR environments could create immersive settings for group readings, allowing users to engage with tea leaf reading in communal spaces that transcend geographical limitations—a delightful realm where practitioners engage in dynamic exchanges around their readings, fostering community through shared experiences.

Additionally, the growth of online platforms and social media dedicated to tasseography presents an exciting opportunity for diverse interpretations to flourish. This version of digital connectivity cultivates an environment where students and enthusiasts alike can explore various methodologies, participate in webinars, and attend workshops that widen their perspectives on symbols and readings. This community-driven aspect of tea leaf reading fosters collaboration and knowledge-sharing, elevating the practice beyond individual interpretations and enriching the collective understanding of the art form.

Another trend is the increasing interest in wellness and self-care through tea leaf reading as practitioners recognize the reflective potential of the practice. In our rapidly changing world, the ritualistic nature of tea leaf readings invites mindfulness, offering a moment of quiet introspection amid chaos. Envisioned as a healing modality, tasseography could take on newfound relevance, especially as more individuals seek holistic approaches to mental well-being. Integrating relaxation techniques, grounding practices, and mindful observations with readings can enhance the therapeutic aspects, allowing tea leaf reading to nurture personal growth beyond traditional interpretations.

As we consider the global reach of tea leaf reading, the influence of diverse cultures will play an essential role in shaping its future trends. The fusion of various traditions and cultural practices into tea leaf readings presents opportunities to discover new symbols and meanings, as well as to revitalize the existing tapestry. Practitioners engaging with these diverse backgrounds can enhance their interpretations, embracing the richness that the considerable interplay of global perspectives offers.

In encouraging creativity and self-expression within the tea leaf reading community, the future is also bright with possibilities. Workshops that invite artistic engagement—be it through sketching, journaling, or other creative outlets—encourage practitioners to explore their emotions freely while documenting their interpretations. This artistic approach integrates personal narratives with tea leaf readings, solidifying the connection between emotional expression and the symbols observed. By blending traditional elements with contemporary creativity, the community nurtures unique pathways for exploration, insight, and connection.

As practitioners reflect on these anticipated trends, it's imperative to approach the adoption of new technologies with appreciation for the practice's roots. Embracing innovation while honoring the cultural heritage of tasseography enables practitioners to create a harmonious balance—ensuring the essence of tea leaf reading remains intact as it grows into new forms. This mindful integration celebrates creativity, collaboration, and personal insight, marking a collective journey into the future of tea leaf reading.

As we anticipate the unfolding chapters of tasseography's evolution, practitioners are invited to remain open to exploration and to engage with the transformative potential of technology as it intersects with tradition. The journey ahead offers rich opportunities—where creativity, community, and innovation converge, allowing practitioners to unveil the potential hidden within every cup of tea. Embracing this exciting future will lead to deeper insights, a sense of connection, and growth within the art of tea leaf reading and its practice as a whole.

17.3. Innovative Integration of Emacs and Divination

Innovative Integration of Emacs and Divination presents a fascinating opportunity for tea leaf readers to marry the art of tasseography with the analytical power of modern technology. Emacs, a highly customizable and extensible text editor, is capable of enhancing the tea leaf reading experience through organization, documentation, and creative expression. As we explore this innovative integration, we uncover how practitioners can utilize Emacs not only to streamline their readings but also to enrich their understanding of the symbols formed by tea leaves, creating a harmonious blend of tradition and modernity.

At the heart of this integration lies the ability to create personalized environments within Emacs tailored specifically for tea leaf reading. Practitioners can set up dedicated files or buffers in Emacs that focus on documenting individual readings. Using Org mode, readers can establish structured logs that record essential details such as the type of tea used, symbols observed, dates of readings, and the emotions associated with each interpretation. This systematic approach empowers readers to maintain a comprehensive archive of their tea leaf readings, facilitating easy access to past insights and enabling them to track their growth and evolution over time.

Moreover, the dynamic capabilities of Emacs allow users to engage in real-time interpretation during readings. By preparing templates or macros that prompt for specific insights or themes while interpreting the leaves, tea leaf readers can document their intuitive responses as symbols emerge. This proactive documentation transforms the reading process into an enlightening and organized exploration, linking emotional intuition with structured analysis. This synergy ensures that readers do not miss significant insights and encourages a holistic engagement with the shapes formed in their cups.

In addition to organizing readings, the integration of visual aids within Emacs can significantly enhance the interpretation process. Practitioners may choose to create drawings or digital sketches of the observed shapes, linking them to established meanings and personal interpretations. Using Emacs as a platform for visual documentation fosters a deeper connection to the symbols, allowing for a creative engagement that enriches the reading experience. By illustrating the shapes alongside notes, practitioners can create a visually engaging reference that brings clarity and depth to their interpretations.

Furthermore, the collaborative possibilities of Emacs offer exciting pathways for community engagement within the tea leaf reading practice. Practitioners can create shared documents where they collectively record insights, interpretations, and unique symbol definitions, fostering a sense of camaraderie and shared learning. This exchange of knowledge nurtures a community where both seasoned readers and newcomers can contribute to an evolving conversation about the meanings that arise from their tea leaves.

Additionally, by creating customizable functions within Emacs for specific readings, practitioners can enhance their interpretative abilities. For example, a function that randomly suggests themes for each tea leaf reading encourages readers to explore new dimensions and encourages a sense of playfulness within the practice. This integrated approach fosters creativity and openness, encouraging practitioners to approach readings with curiosity while documenting their findings systematically.

As the digital landscape continues to evolve, the integration of AI and machine learning into applications utilized alongside Emacs opens even further opportunities. Envision a scenario where advanced analytical tools can analyze previous tea leaf readings, track recurring symbols, and suggest personalized insights based on a user's history. Such innovations would add a layer of depth to the reading process, allowing practitioners to engage with the tea leaves dynamically and intuitively.

In conclusion, the innovative integration of Emacs and divination presents tea leaf readers with expansive opportunities to deepen their practice while respecting the traditions of tasseography. By harnessing the organizational power of Emacs, documenting insights, utilizing visual aids, and engaging with community dynamics, practitioners can transform their relationship with tea leaf readings. As they embrace these advancements, readers open themselves to the potential for transformative insights, enriching their journeys of self-discovery through the mystical art of tea leaf reading.

The integration of Emacs with tasseography not only sustains the art form but also breathes new life into the practice, ensuring that tea leaf reading remains a vibrant, evolving exploration of human experience, intuition, and insight.

17.4. Global Spreads: International Trends

In recent years, there has been a notable surge in interest surrounding tea leaf reading, transcending ancient traditions as it harmonizes with modern practices and technologies. As practitioners from diverse backgrounds engage with tasseography, the dynamics of tea leaf reading continually evolve, incorporating new methodologies and interpretations while honoring the art's rich history. This subchapter delves into global trends in tea leaf reading, reflecting on international influences, cultural exchanges, and the pervasive embrace of this mystical practice worldwide.

One striking trend is the increasing globalization of tea culture, as nations around the world explore and appreciate the rituals tied to tea consumption. In countries such as China, Japan, and India, tea has long been revered not only for its flavors but also for its spiritual significance. As tea practices worldwide converge, the practice of tasseography finds itself at the nexus of cultural exchanges that enrich interpretations and symbolism. Readers from different backgrounds can share their unique perspectives on symbols, drawing from centuries of tea traditions. This blending of cultures allows for a more diverse interpretation of common symbols, creating an expansive landscape of understanding that nurtures communal growth.

As tea leaf readings reach international audiences, an appreciation for the art form's therapeutic potential has emerged. The practice has increasingly been viewed not merely as a means of divination, but also as a holistic approach to mindfulness and self-reflection. With the growing emphasis on mental health and well-being, tea leaf reading offers individuals an opportunity to tap into their intuition and emotional responses, guiding them toward clarity and personal insight. Workshops and classes tend to incorporate mindfulness practices alongside traditional teachings of tasseography, inviting participants to explore their readings through meditative exercises that encourage deeper emotional engagement.

Additionally, the digital age has ushered in unprecedented access to tea leaf reading resources. Online platforms, social media, and virtual communities facilitate ongoing dialogue among practitioners, leading to a collective exploration of techniques and interpretations. As individuals share their readings, insights, and experiences, they contribute to the ever-expanding lexicon of tasseography, reflecting a tapestry of understanding that honors both individual interpretations and the shared wisdom of the community. This interconnectedness fosters a sense of unity among practitioners, reinforcing the notion that the art of tea leaf reading transcends borders and cultural boundaries.

Moreover, the intersection of technology and tea leaf reading has opened exciting avenues for innovation. The rise of apps and platforms dedicated to tea leaf interpretation, along with the community sharing of readings, enhances the accessibility of this ancient practice. Practitioners are harnessing tools that complement their readings while maintaining the traditional rituals tied to tasseography. Whether through comprehensive databases of symbols, digital documentation, or online tutorials, technology enables individuals to enhance their understanding of tea leaves and encourages exploration of the practice's depth and significance.

As interest in tea leaf reading grows, so does awareness of the ethical considerations surrounding the practice. Practitioners increasingly recognize the importance of respecting cultural contexts and traditions, ensuring that contemporary interpretations are imbued with recognition for the past. This consciousness fosters a sense of responsibility among readers to uphold the integrity of tasseography, as they navigate the intricate dance between tradition and modernity.

Ultimately, global trends in tea leaf reading reflect a vibrant synthesis of old and new, embodying the essence of cultural exchange, community engagement, and innovative practices. The evolving landscape invites practitioners to explore a multitude of interpretations and techniques while nurturing connections to their own cultural heritage and those of others. As tea leaf reading continues to grow and adapt, it promises to illuminate pathways toward self-discovery, clarity, and personal insight—allowing the whispers of the leaves to resonate deeply with a diverse array of individuals across the globe.

This collective exploration encapsulates the essence of tea leaf reading, inviting practitioners to engage with the potent symbolism contained within tea leaves while forging deeper connections to their own journeys and narratives. The future of tasseography is undeniably promising, as its integration into modern contexts expands the horizons of participants and ensures the enduring relevance of this ancient practice.

17.5. Encouraging Creativity and Expression

In the rich tradition of tea leaf reading, or tasseography, encouraging creativity and expression serves as an essential component in enriching the practitioner's experience. This chapter emphasizes the importance of fostering a culture of creativity within the practice, allowing tea leaf readers to access deeper insights and interpretations while engaging with the symbolic language of the leaves. The interplay between individual expression and the communal nature of tea readings invites practitioners to explore innovative ways to interact with the mystical elements of tasseography.

At its core, tea leaf reading invites practitioners to tap into their intuitive faculties, bridging the logical with the artistic. By embracing creative expression during readings, individuals can cultivate a deeper connection with the symbols formed by the leaves, enhancing their reflective processes and personal interpretations. Encouraging imaginative engagement not only enriches the reading experience but also fosters emotional resonance, allowing readers to delve into the multifaceted meanings and narratives hidden within the shapes.

One potent way to encourage creativity is through the integration of artistic practices. Practitioners might consider incorporating sketching, painting, or journaling into their tea leaf readings. This artistic engagement serves as a channel for personal expression and reflection, inviting readers to visualize the symbols observed. By illustrating the shapes formed by tea leaves, practitioners deepen their emotional connection to the readings and can uncover insights that may transcend traditional interpretations. Art becomes an extension of the practice, blending intuition and creativity into a harmonious journey of exploration.

A collaborative environment enhances the expression of creativity in tea leaf readings. Workshops, group readings, and community events provide practitioners with opportunities to engage with one another, share their interpretations, and exchange artistic insights. These gatherings foster a spirit of camaraderie and connection, allowing readers to approach their practice with openness and curiosity. Collaborative discussions can yield rich exchanges, where individuals explore new interpretations of symbols and contribute to a collective understanding of the art.

In addition to community engagement, practitioners can utilize digital tools like Emacs to help capture creative insights and enhance expression. By creating organized spaces for documenting readings, sketching symbols, and reflecting on personal interpretations, readers weave a tapestry of experiences that depict their journeys in tea leaf reading. Emacs enables individuals to blend their artistic endeavors with systematic documentation, encouraging exploration of the symbols while nurturing self-expression.

Moreover, incorporating themes of storytelling into tea leaf readings can foster creativity and personal connection. Encouraging practitioners to share narratives associated with their readings—whether anecdotal experiences, emotional responses, or insights inspired by the symbols—invites a deeper dialogue with the teacup. This narrative-driven approach enhances engagement with the symbols, allowing readers to connect their life stories to the shapes formed by the leaves. Research and exploration into storytelling techniques can enrich the reading experience, providing a framework for personal expression set against the backdrop of the tea leaves' whispering secrets.

Finally, it's essential to celebrate moments of creativity, recognizing that all interpretations are uniquely personal. Encouraging practitioners to appreciate their individual journeys fosters a spirit of exploration—thereby allowing readers to break free from rigid interpretations and embrace the fluidity of meaning. By embracing creative exploration, practitioners can cultivate resilience and adaptability in their practice, welcoming the unexpected insights that may emerge from the leaves.

In summary, promoting creativity and expression in tea leaf reading enriches the experience and invites practitioners to explore a multi-dimensional journey filled with personal insights and emotional resonance. By integrating artistic practices, engaging with community, utilizing digital tools, and embracing storytelling techniques, readers create a dynamic tapestry woven from their experiences. Ultimately, each reading becomes an opportunity for creative expression, unveiling profound insights and connections to the symbolic world of tasseography. As practitioners nurture their journeys with curiosity and imagination, they discover that the leaves hold not only messages but also a canvas upon which they can paint their narratives of self-discovery and growth.

18. Conclusion: Embracing Change & Unveiling Potentials

18.1. Reflections on Tradition & Progress

Reflections on Tradition & Progress invites us to contemplate the unique journey tea leaf reading has traversed, from its historical roots steeped in cultural significance to its contemporary rejuvenation as a tool for introspection and self-discovery. Tasseography, with its rich tapestry of meanings and symbols derived from the patterns formed by tea leaves, serves as a profound reflection of our collective human experience, embodying the ancient wisdom while seamlessly integrating with the modern context in which we live today.

Throughout this exploration, we have gained insights into the historical significance of tea leaf reading and the diverse cultural influences that have shaped its practice. The traditions that underpin tasseography remind us of its historical relevance, connecting us to generations of readers who have engaged with the leaves as a means of reflection, guidance, and understanding. These foundational practices grounded in culture and heritage enrich our experience as we embark on our unique journeys, ensuring that we remain rooted in the shared legacies of those who have come before us.

As we examine the progress made in the realm of tea leaf reading, we see that the integration of technology and modern methodologies enhances the accessibility of this ancient art form. Practitioners now harness digital tools to engage with their readings, document insights, and share experiences across global platforms. This modern engagement transforms the practice from an isolated experience into a vibrant community of tea leaf enthusiasts who come together to explore, learn, and grow collectively. As we embrace technology while honoring tradition, we open new pathways for understanding and insight, nourishing our practice with contemporary resources while remaining connected to its rich historical roots.

In reflecting on the balance between tradition and progress, we recognize that personal growth lies at the heart of tea leaf reading. This practice is not merely about interpreting the shapes formed by leaves; it is a journey of self-exploration, nurturing emotional awareness, and encouraging insight. By engaging thoughtfully with the tea leaves, practitioners become attuned to their inner narratives, allowing for a deeper understanding of their lives and experiences. This process of self-discovery cultivates resilience, adaptability, and clarity, empowering readers to embrace the uncertainty of life's journey with confidence and intention.

As we journey forward, we encourage ongoing innovation and adaptation within the practice of tea leaf reading. The evolution of this art form invites us to embrace creativity, develop our intuitive skills, and remain open to new ideas and interpretations. Crafting personalized tools, collaborating with fellow practitioners, and experimenting with techniques enhance our connection to the tea leaves while enriching our experiences in the practice.

However, amid these innovations, we must remain vigilant in balancing skepticism with belief. Embracing tea leaf reading as a source of insight does not require blind faith; instead, it calls for a reflective engagement that allows for the coexistence of intuition and rational thought. Acknowledging the interplay between these aspects fosters an enriched reading experience, where practitioners can fully explore the mysteries revealed within the leaves while remaining grounded in their own discernment.

In conclusion, we extend an invitation for you to embark on your unique path of tea leaf reading with curiosity and open-mindedness. As you delve into the practice, may you recognize the profound transformation that awaits within each cup. Whether through the reflections of tradition, the embrace of innovation, or the connections forged in community, the art of tasseography offers a lens through which to explore the depths of self and the stories that unfold along the journey. Embrace change, honor the legacies of the past, and let the whispers of the tea leaves guide you toward newfound insights and wisdom in your life. Your exploration begins now—may it be a journey of discovery, creativity, and inspiration.

18.2. Harnessing Personal Growth and Discovery

In the realm of tea leaf reading, or tasseography, champions of personal growth and discovery turn to the ancient art as a means of self-exploration and introspection. This practice serves not only as a potent tool for divination, but also as a transformative experience that invites practitioners to delve into their own inner worlds and reveal the layers of meaning inscribed in their lives. Harnessing personal growth within the context of tea leaf readings involves recognizing the significance of the symbols that emerge from the leaves, connecting them to one's life narrative, and allowing the readings to illuminate pathways for development and insight.

As practitioners prepare their tea, setting intentionality becomes paramount. Clarity about what one aims to explore during the reading —be it emotions, relationships, aspirations, or personal challenges— can shape the insights gained from the symbols. This clear focus creates a foundation for reflecting upon the findings of a reading, encouraging individuals to approach the shapes formed in the cup with openness, curiosity, and self-compassion.

The shapes themselves serve as mirrors, revealing emotions and desires that may have previously laid dormant. In observing symbols such as hearts, keys, or crescents, practitioners might find echoes of their own experiences surfacing—enabling them to engage with their thoughts and feelings on a deeper level. The intuitive nature of tasseography invites practitioners to embrace these moments of self-discovery, allowing tea leaves to guide them toward acknowledgment and understanding of their emotional landscapes.

To further harness personal growth, individuals can maintain journals that document their tea leaf readings. Using a platform such as Emacs, readers can create structured entries that encompass the tea type, date, symbols observed, interpretations, and emotional responses. This ongoing record allows practitioners to track their evolution across readings, revealing patterns and insights related to their personal journeys. By engaging in this reflective documentation, individuals can meticulously unravel the complexities of their interactions with the tea leaves, fostering deeper connections to the symbols and enhancing their intuitive skills over time.

Engagement with tea leaf reading should not be confined to solitary practice; fostering a sense of community around the art is equally important. Participating in workshops, group readings, or online forums creates opportunity for shared exploration of personal growth through tasseography. Collaborative experiences allow practitioners to discuss their interpretations and insights, gaining diverse perspectives that nurture understanding and inspire new trains of thought. This communal engagement fosters a vibrant environment that reminds readers that they are part of a larger tapestry of human experience, enriching their understanding of the symbols encountered.

Moreover, unwavering engagement with the evolving nature of tea leaf reading invites practitioners to stay open to innovation in their interpretations. Embracing new perspectives—whether through artistic expressions, technologies, or cultural insights—broadens their relationship with the leaves and enhances their reading abilities. As readers explore alternative methods within the practice, they uncover fresh meanings and dimensions to familiar symbols, transforming each encounter with the leaves into an opportunity for growth.

Encouragement for practitioners to innovate within their practice heightens their personal development journey through tea leaf reading. This may manifest as crafting personalized tools, exploring additional creative modalities, or exploring how the practice can be amplified through tech-driven communities. Allowing oneself to experiment, while simultaneously establishing a strong foundation within the rich legacy of tasseography, nurtures an environment conducive to self-discovery and insight.

In conclusion, harnessing personal growth and discovery through tea leaf reading encapsulates a dynamic interplay of self-reflection, emotional engagement, community interaction, and innovative adaptability. This practice invites individuals to engage with their journeys intimately, using the symbols formed by tea leaves as guides along the path of self-exploration. As tea leaf readers immerse themselves in this enriching journey, they open doors to deeper understanding, promoting personal transformation that weaves together the timelessness of tradition with the ever-present potential for growth and discovery. Each cup becomes a canvas for exploration, inviting readers to unveil the secrets hidden within, leading to profound insights and enriching connections with their identities and the world around them.

18.3. Encouraging Innovation and Adaptation

Encouraging innovation and adaptation is vital in the evolving world of tea leaf reading, a practice steeped in ancient tradition yet ripe for contemporary exploration. As we delve into the art of tasseography, we find that the ability to innovate opens avenues for deeper connection, personal growth, and enriched experiences. Practitioners are encouraged to blend established techniques with new ideas, enhancing the ritualistic beauty of tea leaf reading while respecting its roots.

Innovating within the practice of tea leaf reading can manifest in various forms, ranging from the tools used to document insights to the methods chosen for interpretation. For instance, practitioners may choose to incorporate modern technology, such as digital journals or applications that facilitate the recording of readings. Utilizing platforms like Emacs not only streamlines the documentation process but also allows for interactive engagement with the symbols and shapes observed in the cup. This adaptability fosters an environment where traditional practices can thrive alongside innovative methodologies.

Moreover, creativity plays an essential role in the innovation of tea leaf reading. Practitioners are encouraged to infuse artistry into their rituals—whether that means sketching the symbols, developing a personal symbol dictionary, or creating visually engaging journals that document insights and interpretations. By blending art with the analytical aspects of tasseography, readers nurture a deeper emotional connection to the shapes formed by the tea leaves, enriching their interpretations and enhancing intuitive abilities.

Collaboration within the community further promotes innovation and adaptation. Engaging in workshops, group readings, and discussions allows practitioners to share their insights, experiences, and interpretations. This exchange fosters an atmosphere of collective learning and growth, capturing a rich diversity of perspectives that influence personal interpretations and invite fresh ideas. The act of sharing interpretations encourages readers to consider alternative viewpoints and approaches, ultimately expanding their understanding of the symbols and enhancing their practice.

The practice of tea leaf reading also thrives on humility—the recognition that all interpretations, whether traditional or innovative, are valid as long as they resonate with the individual's journey. By remaining open to new insights and approaches, practitioners encourage a spirit of exploration that embodies growth and adaptability, paving the way for the evolution of tea leaf reading into the future.

As practitioners navigate this evolving landscape, it is essential to strike a balance between skepticism and belief. While it is crucial to embrace innovation, maintaining a critical lens ensures that the essence and integrity of the practice remain intact. Skepticism can serve as a valuable tool that encourages self-reflection and analysis, ensuring that interpretations are thoughtfully considered rather than accepted without scrutiny. This ongoing dance between skepticism and belief fosters a deeper engagement with the practice, where intuition is honored alongside thoughtful reasoning.

In conclusion, encouraging innovation and adaptation within the practice of tea leaf reading invites practitioners to explore new dimensions of meaning while honoring the legacies of tradition. By merging creativity with analytical thought, fostering community engagement, and balancing skepticism with belief, readers enhance their connection to the symbols formed by tea leaves and the insights they yield. Embracing this innovative spirit empowers tea leaf readers to shape their unique journeys in tasseography—an invitation to continue exploring, discovering, and celebrating the wisdom contained within each cup as they navigate the extraordinary art of tea leaf reading.

18.4. Balancing Skepticism and Belief

Balancing skepticism and belief is a nuanced conversation in the world of tea leaf reading and tasseography, serving as a framework through which practitioners can examine their experiences and interpretations. As individuals engage with the symbols formed by tea leaves, they often find themselves traversing the fine line between doubt and faith, which can enrich the reading process while also challenging their approaches. This interplay is essential for fostering a deeper understanding of tea leaf reading as both an art and a reflective practice.

Skepticism in tea leaf reading invites an analytical perspective, encouraging practitioners to question their interpretations and critically evaluate the messages conveyed by the leaves. This mindset serves to prevent the pitfalls of blindly accepting readings that may not resonate with personal truths. A healthy dose of skepticism fosters discernment, allowing individuals to navigate their readings thoughtfully and ensure that they remain grounded in their own lived experiences. As tea leaf readers document their observations and reflect on their insights over time, they can identify patterns and draw connections that reinforce the credibility of their intuitive capacities.

On the other hand, belief in the practice of tasseography nurtures openness and receptivity. Embracing the notion that tea leaves carry messages waiting to be uncovered ignites curiosity and encourages practitioners to explore the deeper meanings behind the symbols. This belief enhances engagement with the reading process, as individuals allow themselves to embrace the mystery and magic woven into the art of tea leaf reading. By cultivating a sense of trust in their interpretations and in the symbolism of the leaves, practitioners can unlock profound insights that may otherwise elude them.

The key lies in finding balance. Readers can approach their tea leaf readings with a keen sense of curiosity and expectation while remaining open to the evolving nature of their interpretations. This balance allows individuals to embrace the lessons gleaned from both skepticism and belief—where critical thinking respects the wisdom of the past while also inviting new perspectives to flourish. The interplay between the two perspectives demands reflection, encouraging practitioners to engage in ongoing dialogues within themselves regarding their readings and the significance of their findings.

Moreover, participating in community discussions reinforces this balance. Engaging with fellow practitioners allows readers to share their experiences and perspectives, promoting the exchange of ideas that may challenge preconceived notions and inspire deeper reflections on their interpretations. By entering a supportive environment where skepticism and belief coexist, readers can cultivate a sense of shared understanding while validating their own journeys.

An essential aspect of balancing skepticism and belief is to allow for a mindful exploration of symbols without imposing rigid expectations. The shapes formed by the tea leaves may not yield immediate clarity or certainty, but they serve as invitations for contemplation and insight. By embracing the ambiguity inherent in readings, practitioners can cultivate resilience and acknowledgment of the journey as an ongoing process, allowing them to celebrate the dynamic nature of interpretations.

In summary, balancing skepticism and belief plays a pivotal role in the practice of tea leaf reading. By adopting a thoughtful approach that appreciates the wisdom of tradition while remaining open to personal exploration, practitioners can unlock the depth of meaning hidden within the leaves. Ultimately, the conversation encourages readers to embrace the interplay of intuition and analysis while navigating their journeys through the symbols, leading to richer insights and self-discovery.

As you consider your own journey in tea leaf reading, may you cultivate the balance between skepticism and belief that resonates with you, enabling your exploration to be a meaningful reflection of your experiences and emotions. This delicate dance invites you to engage fully with the whispers of the tea leaves, uncovering the profound insights that await within each cup.

In closing, we extend an invitation for you to embark on your unique path with curiosity as you delve into the world of tea leaf reading. Embrace the opportunities for self-discovery, personal growth, and awareness that lies in the symbolism of the leaves. Understanding that your interpretation of tea leaves is both an art and a journey allows you to navigate this practice with openness, inviting rich insights and profound connections along the way. Your exploration of tasseography begins now—may it lead you to remarkable revelations, deeper understanding, and a sense of harmony with yourself and the world around you.

18.5. An Invitation to the Journey Ahead

In the enchanting world of tea leaf reading, or tasseography, you stand at the precipice of insight and exploration, ready to delve into a practice steeped in tradition, intuition, and personal discovery. As you embark on this journey, remember that it is not merely about deciphering the patterns left in your cup, but rather about engaging with the stories they tell—stories that reflect your experiences, emotions, and aspirations.

Tea leaf reading offers a profound opportunity for self-exploration. Each time you engage with the leaves, you open yourself up to a dialogue with your subconscious, inviting revelations and insights that can illuminate your path in ways you may have never imagined. Whether you're seeking clarity in relationships, guidance in decision-making, or a deeper understanding of your emotions, the art of tasseography serves as a powerful tool to explore the complexities of your life.

As you begin this transformative journey, allow yourself to cultivate a mindset of curiosity and openness. Embrace the symbols that emerge with wonder, knowing that each shape carries layers of meaning waiting to be uncovered. The dance between logic and intuition, the interplay of creativity and analysis—these elements are what make your readings a unique and enriching experience. It's this intricate balance that can inform more than just interpretations, enabling you to provide a soulful perspective on various aspects of life.

Engage with the community of fellow practitioners, sharing your insights and learning from others. The connections you foster with like-minded individuals enrich your understanding of tea leaf reading, grounding your practice in a supportive network of shared experiences. By participating in workshops, discussions, or online forums, you create a space where collaboration thrives, allowing each person's interpretation to add depth to the collective wisdom of the community.

Utilize modern technology to enhance your practice, harnessing tools like Emacs to document your insights, analyze patterns, and reflect on your growth. These digital aids not only organize your readings but invite creative expressions that will deepen your engagement with the symbols formed by the tea leaves. Let these tools become your companions in the search for deeper meaning as you navigate your personal journey through the lens of tasseography.

Ultimately, tea leaf reading is a dynamic journey of self-discovery and connection that weaves past and present into a tapestry of insights. With each cup, you awaken something within yourself—a sense of intuition, a spark of creativity, a desire for understanding. Embrace this art as a pathway to empowerment, opening your heart to the whispers of wisdom held within the leaves.

As you embark on your own tea leaf reading adventures, may you cultivate a sense of wonder and connection with the symbols that unfold before you. Allow your readings to inspire not just momentary reflections but lasting growth—a journey where every shape carries the potential for insight, and every cup invites you to explore the intricacies of life itself. The path ahead is yours to traverse, filled with opportunities for discovery and self-awareness. Welcome to the art of tasseography; your journey begins now.